All the *Way* Book

Mavis J. Bristow

MAVIS JOANNE BRISTOW

Danielle Jaye Bristow

Tellwell Talent
www.tellwell.ca

ISBN
978-0-2288-4520-1 (Paperback)
978-0-2288-4519-5 (eBook)

Table of Contents

Dedication

I wish to dedicate this book to my family: my husband George, my children and grandchildren, and my sisters and brothers. And also to the people of Strongfield, Loreburn, Elbow and area, who are like family. All have supported me and applauded my accomplishments in every area of my life.

Preface

Gerri's Words

"Have you seen the new teacher in Strongfield play ball? Impressive! She throws that ball as good as any man!" That was the latest news around our small Saskatchewan town and nearby communities after Mavis (Keebaugh) Bristow moved in. There was something about this young woman that made me want to get to know her, and later on I did! She had the ability to impress and surprise everyone, but even more so after the accident that rendered her paraplegic. Although she lost the use of her legs, she found mobility in a wheelchair that neither defined nor confined the strong, determined woman in it.

A challenge served as a new beginning and it was never in her mind to give up without finding a way, like driving her husband George's truck using a baseball bat to reach the accelerator and brake pedals when it was the only vehicle in the driveway. She would also drive the snowmobile or her hand bicycle, take meals to the men in the field on her own, direct the children's choir, bake hundreds of tarts and cookies for bake sales, put up wallpaper, pull herself up the stairs on her behind to get into a friend's house, and travel for caring visits with her mother. She fulfilled her desires to have two more children, to become a lay minister in her church, and do and go to everything everyone else did.

"I can't" was not in her vocabulary. Her attitude remained positive through all the daily trials and tests we all face, but which for her meant finding a way to work through or solve it. Like the time she dropped me off at the mall (for some reason the wheelchair was in the trunk that day) and I jumped out to go shopping, later thinking, *Oh no, I never got the chair out for Mavis and she'll never ask anyone for help!* I ran back, looking to see if the car was in the parking lot. It was, and she wasn't in it. She had asked a parking attendant to get the chair out for her. When we met later, she forgave me and we laughed. I told her, "I never think of the chair. I forget you need it because I never see it when you're in it!"

Mavis: the amazing, wonderful woman I have come to know, love, admire, appreciate and call my friend!

– Gerri Vollmer

Lynda's Words

I first met Mavis one sunny day in June 1974. My husband and I were coming to Strongfield to be new teachers at the school. We weren't married yet, but soon would be. We were driving around the town checking out houses for the fall. We happened to drive past Mavis and George's house. Mavis was outside in her wheelchair pitching balls to her six-year-old son, Donald. Little did I know that day that this lady and I would become dear friends for the next forty-six years. We were neighbours who were close friends as well, and we visited back and forth. We were there for each other in our small rural Saskatchewan village. We shared good times and some not so good times. We laughed a lot and always found much to do. Mavis became a trusted friend and advisor to me after my mom passed away. I could always go to talk with her, and she always welcomed me, no matter how busy she was: making cookies, working on a sermon for Sunday or looking after her grandchildren. Mavis was always there when I needed her. We shared many ideas, planned many events and solved the world's problems on many occasions around her kitchen table. Many times, Mavis would inspire me. She lived life to its fullest. I have so many rich memories of times we have spent together. Thank you for being such a great friend and neighbour all these years!

– Lynda Colton

All the Way

You created every part of me; you put me together in my mother's womb. I praise you because you are to be feared; all you do is strange and wonderful. I know it with all my heart. When my bones were being formed, carefully put together in my mother's womb, when I was growing there in secret, you knew that I was there—you saw me before I was born. The days allotted to me had all been recorded in your book, before any of them ever began.

– Psalm 139:13–16

Chapter One

Childhood

We got up to a gentle rain on a spring Saturday morning. It was the kind of rain that a farmer loves to see after getting the crop in. We decided it was a good day to drive into Saskatoon. We could stop in to see my mom and maybe do a little shopping. Before we returned home, we stopped at our son's house. The sun was bright. His two young boys were happy to be outside as we visited for a short time on their driveway. The youngest one was splashing in a fresh puddle from the morning rain and his older brother was doing tricks to entertain us on his bike. He was riding his bike and showing off. He rode by as we watched from the driveway, stood up on the crossbar of the bike and put his leg out so that he was balancing on the other leg. His face broke into a huge smile from ear to ear, beaming with pride as he showed us his skill.

My memory went back to my own childhood. I remembered doing similar tricks and how I loved to get a laugh or a smile, or just a rise out of someone. I couldn't help but smile at my grandson because it brought back memories from my own adolescence back in Preeceville, Saskatchewan.

How I loved sports. My favourite was softball. At the first sign of bare ground in the spring it was time to get out my bat, ball and glove. I hoped there would be someone around who would like to play catch, or maybe we could bat out some flies. I was so excited. The spring air was cool, but it didn't dampen my excitement about the impending season, or a game of scrub or 500. There were many friends around that were as excited as I was—well, almost!

I would hurry through my lunch and then back to our nearby school. Out to the back alley I would run, taking my ball and glove with me, and over to the big brick schoolhouse that was only about a block and a half away. I'd hear other kids in the schoolyard, glad to be outside. I would hurry to find my friends, Betty-Jean or Dean. They loved to play ball as much as I did. At the ringing of the school bell we all headed into class, but my thoughts were on the ball game we would have after school.

When school was out we rushed home and gathered across the road in the Canadian National Railway lot where we made our ball diamond. We would start out playing scrub, but it wouldn't be long before more friends would come and we'd be able to choose sides to get a game going. Dean was often one of the captains, and it pleased me that I was often the first one he chose to be on his team. He was a good athlete, and when he chose me it meant that he thought I was a good ball player. How good that made me feel!

At suppertime we would all go home, but we were back not long after eating to resume our game. I made sure that when we had to clean up after supper or lunch that I chose to do the breakfast dishes. That made me free for the rest of the day.

Organized sport was something that was never heard of when we grew up. We organized our own sports and always had lots of kids out to play.

When ball season was over, which went for most of the summer, we got into football. Boys and girls both played: Betty-Jean, Norman, Dean, Clair, me—the whole gang! We gathered at the schoolgrounds after school to play football. My special girlfriend, Betty-Jean, also loved sports. We would gather with the boys for a rough and tough game of football. I loved to catch a long pass while on the run. I would watch over my shoulder as Dean threw me a long bomb, and I'd grab it and run for the touchdown. We took turns playing offence and defence. We would tackle the boys and they would tackle us. The gender didn't matter. My dad didn't like me playing this rough, and I was told many times that it wasn't a "girl's game." I knew if I was caught I would be scolded, so at about five o'clock, when Dad would be coming home from work at the local grain elevator, I would watch for his car. When I saw it, I would duck behind the school until he went by, and then back out on the field I would hurry, not missing a play. Betty-Jean got opposition from her mother, Mrs. Patterson, a classy little woman with a very Scottish accent. She did her best to dress Betty-Jean in frills and lace. Mrs. Patterson was a very talented, artistic lady. She painted beautiful pictures and sewed pretty little dresses for Betty-Jean. For the local carnival in town she would dress Betty-Jean up like Shirley Temple to ride on the float, with ringlets and bows in her hair. After a few broken brassiere straps Betty-Jean gave up the game, but her mother may have had something to do with her early retirement from football. It took some stern warnings from the high school principal and a badly twisted knee to make me give up this rough sport, but I would still often play catch with a football.

Winter months would find me tobogganing on the hill next to our house that crossed the road and went down to the platform at the railway station. We were forbidden to be on the hill when the train came in. It was a busy place: trucks and cars and the town dray, a kind of delivery cart. Boxes were unloaded off the train and onto the dray to be taken to local businesses in town. I remember that the dray was once pulled by two horses, but later by a little tractor and then a truck. Many hours were spent sliding down that hill in the wintertime, as once again kids from all around town came with their sleds and toboggans. I even remember a bright red bobsled that several would jump on, and down the hill we would go. One time one of the younger kids was hurt when we hit a telephone pole at the side of the road, but fortunately not too badly.

Fun on the hill wasn't our only activity. Like most small towns the local skating and curling rinks were busy places. The rinks were several blocks from our house, but we would bundle up and head over to skate. I wasn't a good skater, and I wore second-hand skates. They were low-cut and had a band of wool around the top. I had weak ankles and the skates didn't have any support, so I would go over on my ankles. Years later I got better skates and enjoyed skating much more. Several years later, in Strongfield, I played goalie for the local women's hockey team.

Dad used to like to curl. How thrilled I was when he asked me to curl with him in the local matches. I was in Grade 5 and one of the younger curlers. I thought that I was the most special kid on the face of the earth! I would often hang around the rink before a draw or after I was done, hoping to be asked to spare.

I will cherish memories of these sporting activities as I grew up in the town of Preeceville for the rest of my life. Once I had grown and left my hometown, the competitive spirit I developed as I participated in sports helped me through all the challenges I was to face.

Chapter Two

∽∽∽

Cheaper by the Dozen?

I saw a movie once when I was growing up called *Cheaper by the Dozen*. I don't imagine my dad, Warner Keebaugh, thought *we* were cheaper by the dozen, but there were twelve in our family. I was always proud of our big brood. I liked to tell my friends that I had seven older brothers and sisters. From all my memories we were a happy family growing up. We didn't have a lot, but we had all we needed. My parents provided well for us and loved each one of us. My dad was married twice. He lost his first wife, Alta, when she was very young, and he was left with seven children. The youngest was only two months at the time my dad's first wife died. He went to live with his grandparents, my dad's mom. Some of my dad's older children did not live at home as I was growing up, but the youngest three I remember well as part of our family.

My twin sister Merla and I were my mother's oldest. Mom met my dad while teaching in Sturgeon River and they were married a few years later. I've often wondered what Dad thought when, two years after he married Mom, they found out they were expecting twins! Within five years three more children had joined the family, and we were twelve.

Merla and I looked very much alike, and most people could not tell us apart. Mom stopped short of saying we were identical, because she *could* tell us apart. We had white-blond hair and blue eyes. Merla was the first born, about ten minutes before me. She was the older and wiser sister. Even though we looked alike we always had different interests. Merla didn't share my interest in sports. She loved music. She and her friend Gloria shared an interest in piano and singing. She was always more serious and more conscientious than I was. She worked hard at her schoolwork and music. She loved nice clothes and was particular about the way she looked. Music was something Mom gave us that we all enjoyed. We were taught piano lessons from our mother and later we went to another music teacher in town. She prepared us for the Royal Conservatory of Music piano exams.

Next to Merla and me was Karen, two and a half years younger. She had darker hair than us, wavy and very pretty. She also had beautiful blue eyes. She was quiet and shy but had the determination to hold her own if she had to. We all seemed to have that Keebaugh determination to be the best we could be. She too was musical and had a lovely sweet voice. Like Merla she was conscientious and always wanted to do well at everything. She had a little more love for sports then Merla, so I could convince her to play ball. We have always teased her about her love for kittens because we remember her dragging home many strays from the neighbourhood. It indicated her soft-heartedness.

Vicki, born in January of 1947, was the next little girl to join our family. Karen and Vicki were only thirteen months apart and have always been close friends. Often people would ask Mom which pair were the twins, Merla and me or Karen and Vicki. Vicki had very curly hair and brown eyes. When we were gathered around the piano for singsongs we would always sing "Beautiful Brown Eyes" by Rosemary Clooney. Vicki liked that song! She didn't have the singing voices that Merla, Karen and I had, but her croaky expression would shout out the words in perfect time. One of Vicki's talents was reciting poetry and she was very good at it, using drama and lots of expression. She was a very good student, and we were always envious of her high marks. I always remember her quoting the following poem for a talent contest in which she received very high marks. Vicki had Mom's love and appreciation of poetry. She became a teacher after finishing school and gained the reputation of being a very good one. Parents did their best to get their children in Vicki's class.

> There was once a rabbit with silver fur,
> Her little grey neighbours looked up to her,
> Till she thought with pride in the moonlit wood,
> "The reason I'm white is because I'm good."
>
> "Oh! what shall I do!" cried a tiny Mole.
> "A Fairy has tumbled into a hole.
> It is full of water and crawly things
> And she can't get out, for she's hurt her wings.
>
> "I did my best to catch hold of her hair,
> But my arms are short, and she's still in there!
> Oh! darling white rabbit, your arms are long.
> You say you're good, and I know you're strong."

"Don't tell me about it!" the Rabbit said;
She shut up her eyes and her ears grew red;
"There's lots of mud, and it's sure to stick,
Because my fur is so long and thick."

"There's plenty of water," the wee Mole cried;
"There are shining rivers from moorlands wild;
Dew from the sky, and the dear grey rain;
And the Fairy to kiss you clean again.

"Oh! dear! Oh! dear!" sobbed the poor little Mole;
"Who will help the fairy out of the hole?"
A common grey Rabbit popped up from the gorse.
"I'm not very strong, but I'll try, of course."

His little tail bobbed, as he waded in;
The muddy water came up to his chin;
But he caught the Fairy tight by the hand,
And sent her off safe into fairy-land.

But she kissed him first on his muddy nose,
She kissed his face and his little wet toes;
And when the day dawned with the early light,
The dirty grey Rabbit was shining white!

I don't know the author of this poem. I believe it was in one
of our elementary school readers. It is one I can recite by memory,
but I was delighted to find it online. I didn't find the name of the
author. I read that the poem was in the context of a play.

Mom would often quote poetry to us or sing us a song that would teach us valuable lessons. A poem like this one was the kind that Mom would often recite to us.

Our little brother Kent was the youngest in the family. Some thought that he might be spoiled, but he would claim that he was always nagged at by four older sisters. Kent was blond with brown eyes. He never took the interest in sports that I did. He was and still is an animal lover, especially of dogs. If Karen brought home stray cats, Kent would find stray dogs. We had a white part–Siberian Husky named Duke that Kent trained to pull our sleigh. Dad found a harness and collar and Kent would hitch Duke up to the toboggan. Duke would pull him all around town. There were some people in town afraid of Duke, but we loved him.

In later years we labelled Kent the "Golden Boy," because Mom would look so forward to him coming home. She looked forward to each of us coming home, but we loved to tease Kent.

Kent and I were always close growing up. I was his protector. In any of our childhood squabbles it was me who would come to his rescue when he felt that his older siblings were picking on him. There were many times that I ran after him down the hill, across the railroad tracks and out into the field. There we would sit and talk or walk on down and sit on the bank of the Assiniboine River in the trees. We would skip stones into the river. Sometimes I'd wrestle him to the ground to calm him when he was upset. We spent many hours out in that field drowning out gophers, or we would get scrap lumber from around Dad's grain elevator and build clubhouses. Dad would sometimes have us do odd jobs around the elevator. Kent and I are alike in one silly way: we both seemed to like to get a rise out of people by saying or doing some crazy thing. Kent still likes to exaggerate some crazy thing or another he did to get a rise out of his sisters, or others.

The five of us spent many happy times playing in a playhouse that Dad built in the backyard. We four girls would get a new doll each Christmas for many years. Kent would often get some sort of riding toy and later tools of some kind. Mom would work late into the night sewing doll clothes that would be under the tree on Christmas morning.

We weren't rich in material things growing up, but we had the necessities and we knew that we were loved. We made our own fun in our backyard or around the community. Dad also built us a swing in the backyard. He put strong four-by-four posts into the ground and got rope to build the swing. I remember we would often wind it around the board on the top until it was very short, then I would hang upside down with my ankles hooked in the rope at the top. We would put on circus acts where I would grab the hands of one of the younger ones and swing. We also created fun performances with our friends and put on shows in our garage, singing songs and reciting poetry. I have memories of Vicki strutting across the floor singing in her raspy voice, "I dreamt that at my coronation, I was queen of all the nation giving up my throne to marry you." She would then fling the scarf she was wearing out into the audience. We often performed in our backyard with and for other kids around the neighbourhood.

Mom and Dad were proud. They provided for our family and they worked hard. There were times when friends wanted us to go to a movie and Mom and Dad didn't have the money to give us to go. Mom would take us aside and instruct us to tell our friends that we didn't want to go and not tell them that we didn't have the money. It was hard, but she would stand by us as we did as we were told.

The words of many songs that she taught us often come to mind: "Oh, we don't have a barrel of money / maybe we're ragged and funny / but we'll travel along, singing a song, side by side . . ." or, "Those were the days my friend / I thought they'd never end / I'd sing and dance forever and a day . . ." or, "Que sera sera . . ." Oh so many wonderful songs that run through my mind.

Mom, Dad and ten of my twelve siblings.

My twin sister Merla and me at age one.

Christmas with siblings.

Chapter Three

Older Siblings

We always thought we were special to have the bonus of older siblings. Dad wanted us to think of ourselves as one big family, not two separate families. My older brother Byron always said we were to introduce him as our brother, not half-brother. Marge and Byron, two of the three youngest children from my dad's first marriage, grew up with us. When we were little, Marge and Byron were a big help to Mom in looking after we younger ones. Marge was also a huge help to Mom in other ways. We have wonderful memories of her taking us skating and cleaning up after meals. She was quick to get the plates cleared off the table and washed up. Marge graduated and went on to become a nurse. We were always very proud of her. She was very tiny, quick to get a job done and fast on her feet. She had the most infectious laugh. When we grew up and had homes of our own, we always enjoyed the times our families got together.

Byron would chop wood in the backyard and pile it neatly along the fence. There was always wood ready to bring in for the stove in the kitchen. Dad often told us about Byron sleepwalking outside to chop wood in the middle of the night. Byron acquired a strong work ethic. He worked at the local printing office, *The Preeceville Progress.* He left home young and apprenticed in the newspaper business in Edmonton. Eventually he bought a local newspaper business in Cut Knife, Saskatchewan, and eventually *The Meridian Booster,* a weekly paper in Lloydminster. He worked hard and became a very successful businessman. I spent some of my summers babysitting for Byron, looking after two of his children. It was a special treat to be at the lake with his family. Later, when he had a home in Arizona, my husband and I spent time with him and his wife in Mesa. We were so proud of him and loved his warm smile and delightful laugh, always welcoming our visit.

Byron carried our drinking water up the hill from a well at the CN station. Later it was my job, and when Kent got older it was his. We each had the chance to do that job, but it was something that I liked to do. I would climb the hill twirling around with two pails of water as fast as I could to see if I could spin fast enough not to spill any water.

Water was heated in the reservoir at the side of the stove for doing dishes and other things. It would also then be ready for our Saturday night bath. Mom had a square tub that she would set in the middle of the kitchen floor and we each took turns having a bath. If you were first, you got fresh warm water. Each person after that got a dipper of hot water in the tub. Imagine not having a morning shower like we are used to today! We often pulled straws to see who would be first. I think that Kent was first most of the time because he was the baby.

Ward was the youngest of my dad's first family. He lived with his grandmother (my dad's mom) and Dad's stepfather until he entered high school in Grade 9. He then came to live with us. How we loved having a big brother around! We looked up to Ward. He was very good to us, his younger siblings.

Dad always made it clear to us that we needed an education so that we could earn our own way in life. Even if we didn't finish school, we needed to get experience in a trade of some kind so that we were able to look after ourselves. We all knew our parents' expectation that we needed to be independent, and we have passed that same expectation on to our families. I have always said that if we don't have any expectation of our children, that is what we will get: nothing! I learned that from my dad.

Ella was the oldest of our family. She didn't seem very close to us when we were young because she moved out on her own before Mom and Dad were married. We got closer to Ella in later years when our families got together. She had two daughters just about our age and we loved to have them come to visit, or we would go to visit them in B.C. They lived in Savona, right beside Kamloops Lake. We thought that was heaven.

Vesta, the second oldest from Dad's first marriage, also left home before Mom and Dad married. She joined the army and went overseas. We never knew Vesta very well. There was the occasional visit, but she chose not to be close to the family. When she came for a visit, she would stay in the Golden West Hotel in Preeceville, not with us—too many excited kids, I guess. Freda and Wayne, the third and fourth children of Dad's first marriage, lived with Mom and Dad for a short time after Mom and Dad were first married. Mom taught Wayne high school in a one-room schoolhouse. Freda went to Edmonton, married and made her home there. We loved to visit Freda in her lovely home. It was built on the side of a ravine with a walk-out basement, and we thought it was a castle. She had lovely white furniture and plush carpets. Wayne went into the army and took commerce. He was a paymaster in the army and he too went overseas. It was always very exciting when Wayne and his wife Jean came home. They would play with us and fuss over us. They would usually bring us a little gift from some special place. I have memories of him and Jean rolling their own cigarettes. We thought they were really high-class! What a difference there is in the opinion of smoking now we are aware of what it does to our health.

After Ward graduated, he went to work for CN Rail. He once came home on the train for a visit, and we were so excited when he retrieved two two-wheeled bikes from the train for us to share. That was a very special gift! We were definitely the luckiest kids in town.

Chapter Four

Dad

Thinking of my early years in Preeceville and growing up in a large family surrounded by love, I remember the special love of my dad and how he worried about his family. It has been many years that he has been gone, so many of my memories have faded. He was a man who earned the greatest respect from each of his children, who loved us all dearly and wanted us each to be educated so we could be independent and earn our own way in life.

We always called him "Daddy." I don't know why; maybe it was because Mom referred to him as "Daddy" when she was speaking of him to us. That was the name we grew up with. I wouldn't say it was a term of endearment, because he wasn't a man I felt close to affectionately. I don't ever remember sitting on his lap, but I probably did when I was little. I remember him holding his grandchildren. He always seemed to have a softness for the little girls, but he was very good to all of them. I do remember our oldest son, Donald, sitting on Granddad's knee. He was a very strict German man and a disciplinarian. Along with my respect for him there was always a certain amount of fear. He spoke crossly, but even though his threats made me fearful, they were usually only threats. I remember his speaking crossly to my brothers also. I only remember one time that he laid a hand on me, and it was for talking disrespectfully to Mom and not backing down when he spoke to me. I felt I was right and was arguing my point. When we spoke back to either Mom or Dad, they made it clear that talking back was unacceptable. Dad's gruffness was usually mostly talk. His bark was much worse than his bite. He had the greatest love and respect for Mom, and he demanded that each of us have love and respect for her as well, and we certainly did.

I wish that over the years I had written down some of his adages, because through his little rules or sayings he taught us many values. Some of them came from the Bible, although we didn't realize it growing up. "Money is the root of all evil," is a good example. Some of them were his own; maybe he got them from his mother. He would often remind us that "blood runs thicker than water." He meant that we should value our family relationships. He wanted his family to be close and to support each other. If he thought that we were spending too much time with friends, he would accuse us of "licking their ears out." He said that your family are the ones you will turn to in a crisis. They are the ones you'll want to depend on.

Another favourite expression was: "If someone can't look you in the eye, they are no good." He believed in dealing honestly with people and that you are "only as good as your word." A handshake would seal a deal. As I grew older and wanted to go out in the evening with friends, he'd insist that I be in by midnight, saying, "Nothing good happens after midnight."

Often he would follow me to the door and say before I left, "Don't do anything that would hurt your mother!" That is all he would have to say.

My father always had a deep fear that something might happen to one of us. One particular activity that he feared was swimming. He was never very anxious to take us to the lake, but we often begged to go swimming. Mom would have to persuade him to take us. As was their custom when we begged to do something, Mom and Dad would go into the bedroom, close the door, and talk it over. When they emerged from their discussion Mom would have persuaded him.

A summer afternoon at the lake was a special treat, and it didn't happen very often. We would all be excited as we piled into the car and headed for nearby Chrystal Lake, about an hour away. There was Nelson Lake nearby also, but he felt that it was dangerous. Before we got near the water, we would get strict instructions that we couldn't go in past our waists. If we did it would be the end of our swimming that day. We were told to wade out to our waist and swim back. Dad would pace back and forth on the beach with a frown etched across his brow, while Mom always seemed to enjoy the water with us. None of us got to be very good swimmers when we were young. Kent later became a very good swimmer and loved it. After what seemed to be a very short time, we would hear Dad say, "That's enough! It's time to get out."

My dad's dad died as a result of falling off a log while riding logs up a river in Michigan. That may have been where his fear of water originated. He couldn't swim himself and never went near the water.

Dad's ancestors came from Germany and settled in Michigan. He was only two years old when his father died. His mother came to homestead in the Shellbrook area with Allan Hulbert, who was the only grandfather we ever knew. Dad and his younger brother were the only two boys. Dad fondly referred to Grandpa Hulbert as "the old man." He had a great deal of love and respect for his mother, and Grandpa Hulbert was always good to her. Dad appreciated that. Our brother Ward, who lived with them for most of his years growing up, once said, "Dad dearly loved three women: his mother, my mother and yours." That was very evident in our dad's life.

Dad was a worrier, and you could always tell if he was upset about something. There would be a frown etched on his forehead, and I will never forget that look—it is the first vision that comes to my mind when I think of him. I can see him standing at the window of our home in Saskatoon, watching me back out of the driveway. He seemed to have that worried look every time he saw me leave for home.

After I left home and became a schoolteacher, I came home for a visit wearing high-heeled shoes with a pointed toe, and he said, "With those shoes you could kick the eye out of a snake."

His words will always stick in my mind. His last words to Kent, his youngest son, were, "Look after your mother." We all took those words very seriously. We loved and cared for her for many years after he passed away. Mom lived to 103 years of age. There is much to share about her life, and I will do that in a later chapter.

Chapter Five

———— ⊗⊗⊗ ————

Track and Field:
A School Highlight

I t was the month of May, sometime in the early fifties. My birthday is in May, but I didn't look forward to it as much as to this day: the local field meet. I was up early and put on the new red T-shirt that I got just for this day, and my navy shorts. All the kids in our school would be dressed the same today. I was anxious to get to school, so I hurried through my breakfast. Mom always insisted we have a good breakfast, because, "It is the most important meal of the day." We never went without breakfast. Everyone was excited about the day. Today it is referred to as "track and field."

Each school in the Sturgis School Unit was dressed in a different colour, because this distinguished which school you went to. All the country schools were bussed into our school in Preeceville. There we lined up in pairs behind our banners, the lowest grades first followed by the older ones. Two students in front carried the banner. I would have loved to have been chosen to carry the banner, but I never was. It felt like the Olympics as we marched from the schoolyard to the sports ground. We had quite a distance to go as we marched from the school, three blocks down past main street, as people lined up to see us march by. We walked on past the United Church and around the corner to the Lutheran church on the next corner overlooking the valley below where the Assiniboine River was. We marched down the hill, past the creamery, over the bridge, past the local cemetery and into the sports ground. It was all groomed and ready for the big day. In the booths around the ground were the parents who volunteered, selling hotdogs, drinks and treats, crispy marshmallow treats and puffed wheat cake.

My best events were usually the jumping contests. Long jump and broad jump were my favourites, but I would go in as many events as I could. I liked the races, but there were a couple of long-legged girls who were better than I was. I usually did well in the throwing events: ball throw and shot put. If we got first, second, third or fourth we would get a red, blue, yellow or white ribbon pinned to our shirts. I was always so proud of those ribbons, blowing in the breeze as I ran across the field.

After lunch it was time for the ball games. This was the highlight of the day. Usually the final game was Preeceville against Sturgis, the two large schools. The ball games were always between these schools. There was a boys' game and a girls' game. The pitcher for the Sturgis girls was very good. She and I were about the same age; therefore, every year of high school we would play against each other. She could smoke a fast strike across the plate. I loved to get a hit off her! I was nicknamed "Slugger McGee" when playing ball. I would stand up at the plate and everyone would be yelling, "C'mon, Slugger, hit that ball!" When the game was over, the day was done. We were dismissed and allowed to go home. School buses would pick up the country children and the town kids would walk home. I would run over the bridge to where some of the kids would wander down to the bank of the river and wade in the water. We were never allowed to do that. Mom and Dad were always afraid of the currents in the river. I'd continue running up the hill and then three blocks down the street to our house.

My face and arms would be red and my freckles in full bloom. A smile would stretch across my face as I proudly displayed my ribbons and talked about our ball game. This was a great day! After I had shown off my ribbons to Mom, I'd run down the hill to see our neighbour, Mrs. Johnson, in the station house. I loved to show her my ribbons also. Mrs. Johnson had a pond with fish in the backyard. We would sit in her beautiful yard and she would give us cookies and milk. Mrs. Johnson had a round, happy face and always made a fuss over us. Mr. Johnson always joked with us also. We thought they were very special.

Chapter Six

Gone Fishing
and Other Adventures

I t was about the mid-fifties, and summer holidays were here. School was done. We got our report cards and we had passed. We looked forward to a visit from our cousins from Saskatoon. Kent was always excited about the cousins coming because there would be boys to play with. Mom's sister, Adell, would let her three youngest, Valerie, Brent and Grant, come and spend a week with us in the summer, and then three of us would spend a week in Saskatoon. We always looked forward to that holiday in the summer. Valerie, Brent and Grant always looked forward to coming to our place and enjoying the activities in the country. The girls took turns with the boys each night sleeping out in the playhouse. The boys would often get up in the morning and go fishing at a nearby creek. One morning when we girls slept out in the playhouse, we decided that we would get up early, take the boys' fishing rods and go fishing. We jumped on the bikes, doubled up in some cases, and off we went to the creek with big plans of catching some fish. We caught a big one, all right! Poor Karen, who was always the quiet one, was standing behind one of us when we cast the rod. It flew back and got caught on the top of her head. Fearing we were in big trouble, we got on our bikes and headed home. Mom had to take Karen to the local hospital to get the fishhook out of her head. That was the end of the girls' fishing trips.

There were other hospital trips that I remember, and Karen was the patient another time. She was standing quietly behind me while I swung a golf club, and I hit her in the head as I swung through. I turned around to see a lump swell up on her forehead and break open. Mom saw it from the kitchen window and rushed out. Blood was streaming down Karen's face. She looked up at Mom with her big blue eyes and said, "Will I die?" Mom and Dad rushed her to the hospital to get stitches. In my enthusiasm for sports, poor Karen was the recipient of my strong swing!

An appendix attack put Vicki in the hospital when she was a little girl. Children weren't allowed to visit in the hospital, but when Mom went to see her, the rest of us would go up and sit on the curb, looking up into the window on the second floor of the hospital and waving at Vicki looking down at us. We thought a week in the hospital was a long time and we missed our little sister.

Chapter Seven

Church Life and Sundays

T he United Church was our church in Preeceville, and our involvement in many social activities was linked to it. We belonged to Canadian Girls in Training (CGIT), the Young People's teenage group and the junior choir. Along with that, we attended Sunday school and church most Sundays. Mom played the piano for the junior choir. We were never allowed to miss choir practice, which was one night a week after school. The junior choir sang almost every Sunday. Merla and Karen sang soprano and I sang alto. I always enjoyed choir practice, because it was something that we always did at home, often on a Sunday afternoon or evening. Sometimes we would play church for Mom and Dad. They were the congregation, but Mom played when we sang. I remember that I liked to be the minister and I would get up and pound on the table. I don't know where I got that idea from—maybe we had a minister who pounded on the pulpit. The only time I ever complained about going to choir practice was if it conflicted with a curling match or a ball game.

Our church services in Preeceville were on Sunday evenings. After church we looked forward to going to the local Chinese restaurant for a pop, and sometimes a bismark à la mode—that was a bread doughnut with jam in the centre. It opened up and there was ice cream inside. That was always a special treat.

Sunday was usually a day of rest for our family. Mom always insisted we get chores done Saturday and then we could play on Sunday. Sunday suppers were two roasted chickens and homemade ice cream. Dad kept big blocks of ice in the garage under wood shavings so that he had ice for the ice-cream maker. He had a farmer keep chickens for him just outside of town, and on Saturday he and Byron—and later Kent—would go and get two chickens. It was their job to kill, pluck and clean them. All I can remember Mom doing was getting the boiling water ready. Dad brought them into the house for Mom to stuff and put in the oven. The girls were not allowed outside when he killed chickens. We had to stay in the house, because killing and cleaning chickens was a man's job in my dad's eyes. Kent would love to tell us about the chickens running around with their heads cut off. We thought he was just making up a story, but eventually found out he was right.

The same group of girls that belonged to the junior choir also belonged to CGIT, so there was a time that the choir was actually the CGIT choir. Our big production in CGIT each year was the Vespers service at Christmas time. It was a candlelit service, and there would be candles all around the church. One year at Vespers, with candles lit in the windows of the church, we girls paraded in wearing our traditional CGIT uniforms, with blouses called "middies"—a white and blue mid-length blouse—and a navy skirt. I was standing at the back of the church against the window and my middy caught on fire from the candle in the window. There was much commotion as the girls swatted me on the back with their books and programs to put out the fire. It could only happen to me!

The youth group, Young People's, also met once a week. Our leader was the same lady who was our choir director, and she was also part of the CGIT leadership. We often had members of the community come to speak to us. Once, our minister, Rev. Thomas, who was East Indian, came to talk to us, and after he spoke we had time to ask questions. We were talking about the topic of death and someone asked him why people die. His answer stuck in my mind for years after. He said, "God puts each of us on the earth with a mission to accomplish. We all have a job to do, and when our job is done he takes us home." The reason it especially stuck in my mind was because Rev. Thomas passed away very shortly after that from a heart attack. It was a big shock to the community. He was very well liked.

I was confirmed in the United Church at fourteen years of age. I took confirmation classes from a very serious, no-nonsense man who was very sincere. Rev. Camidge was a single man when he was in Preeceville. He took the confirmation classes very seriously. There was no goofing around in his sessions. This was hard for me. I was always looking for a laugh and would usually do something to get other kids going. I remember one time in particular when I was actually being serious, but Rev. Camidge didn't realize that I was, as my reputation preceded me. He asked us how we were to prepare for communion, and I told him that we would have to wash the communion glasses.

The other kids giggled, and he told me to leave the class. I sat outside beside the church and waited for the others to come out. I didn't dare go home early without Merla, because I knew my parents would ask why I was home earlier than she was. I was confirmed with the class, even though I don't think I was very mature in my thinking. Merla picked out dresses for our confirmation. Her dress was blue with big black flowers and mine was the same style, only in red. For many years I thought about that incident and wondered why Rev. Camidge was so upset about my answer to his question. I thought that washing the glasses was a perfectly logical thing to do. I felt badly about being asked to leave the class, but I never let on to the others. This was something I pondered many times.

My years growing up in Preeceville were happy. We had a contented, innocent childhood. My sisters, Kent, and sometimes friends enjoyed fun in the playhouse that our dad built for us. We had a homemade swing that he built. We had friends around our neighbourhood who loved sports in winter and summer, and we had music in our family, church and community. Mom often taught us valuable life lessons by reciting poetry to us. I can't remember Mom and Dad having many disagreements. If there was something they wanted to discuss, they would go into the bedroom and close the door. When they came out they would have come to a decision about a certain subject that they would then share if it concerned one of us. It was very rare that our parents weren't in our home, but I remember silly games that we would play with each other when they were away. I remember how we would turn all the lights out when Mom and Dad were away, take off our pajamas, throw them out in the middle of the floor, then run out in the dark, grab some and put them on. When we turned on the lights we would giggle away at the mixed-up pajamas that we ended up wearing. It was simple, innocent fun. We never saw alcohol in our home or experienced abuse of any kind. We were loved and valued, and even though we didn't have a lot, we had the necessities and we knew that Mom and Dad loved us.

Chapter Eight

Leaving Preeceville Behind

My childhood years growing up in Preeceville were wonderful, happy times. They are years that I look back on and fondly cherish.

In 1961 my dad retired from Searle Grain as an elevator agent. Merla and I were eighteen years old. My mother was hired in Saskatoon at Prince Philip School as a Grade 1 teacher. Mom and Dad had a house built in Saskatoon and we moved that summer. We all left behind many friendships.

Merla graduated from Grade 12, and I should have too, but I missed three of my twelfth-grade subjects, mainly because my interest in the spring of the year was playing ball rather than studying. I felt really bad, but I was allowed to take part in the graduation ceremony, although I didn't receive my diploma. We went shopping in Yorkton for graduation dresses. Merla picked out two light blue dresses and shoes to match. We were identical! It didn't bother me to let her pick out dresses because I really wasn't that interested in them, and she was actually the one graduating, not me.

After the graduation exercises there was a party at Nelson Lake, and of course our dad did not want us to go to it. Because I was more interested in the party and more rebellious, I snuck out my bedroom window that night and went to the party. When I returned later and tapped on the window, Merla helped me back inside. To my knowledge, my parents never knew of my adventure that night. The party was a wiener and marshmallow roast. There may have been alcohol around that night, but I didn't have any of it. It was never a part of our fun times in Preeceville. The only time I can remember trying alcohol there was tasting home brew outside the Ukrainian Catholic Hall at the west end of town during a wedding dance. I was hanging around with Betty-Jean, Dean, Clair, and Merla, and probably others. It was terrible-tasting stuff. Maybe that was my cure for ever wanting alcohol!

Because I did not have my Grade 12 diploma, I decided I would put my name in at the Toronto Dominion Bank and apply for work in the fall. My mother and her sister, Aunt Doree, felt I should go back to school and complete my Grade 12. I felt embarrassed about going to a big school in the city to repeat three subjects, but Aunt Doree knew the principal of Aden Bowmen Collegiate and arranged for me to have an interview with him.

In September of 1961 I went off to Aden Bowmen to repeat the three subjects and take three extra subjects. Every morning I walked eight blocks to Aden Bowmen Collegiate, and Vicki and Karen walked eight blocks the other direction to Walter Murray Collegiate. Kent was still in elementary school about three blocks away, and Mom often drove him on her way to Prince Philip.

I enjoyed my year at Aden Bowman and met several friends. We had to wear dresses to school in those years, and I remember pulling long, heavy stockings up, or wearing pants under our skirts to head off to school on cold winter mornings. I enjoyed taking part in some sports that I hadn't played before, like volleyball and basketball. I never did very well in basketball because of my aggressiveness—I often fouled out early in the game. I also really enjoyed curling on the Aden Bowman girls' team, but felt really badly when I wasn't allowed to play in the senior girls' playoffs because I was a year older. I had been chosen to skip the team and then was told that I was too old.

At Aden Bowman I became friends with a girl whom I still keep in touch with, Maureen (Fearer) Marble. We often got in trouble for goofing around in home economics classes or chemistry labs. Maureen was a pretty girl with dark hair and big brown eyes. I can still picture her doubled up in laughter after some of our silly antics. To this day we laugh about some of the things we did. The chemistry lab was built belowground, and the windows opened right at ground level. One time the window was open in the room—it was spring and there was still snow on the ground. I was working beside the open window, and I reached out and got a handful of snow. I threw a snowball that flew between two Bunsen burners and hit Maureen right on the cheek. She looked over and started laughing. I started to laugh also. I don't know why we never got in trouble, but we laugh to this day about how accurate my throw was. We also laugh about some of our sewing in home economics, our bound buttonholes and welt pockets. Although I was never very good in home economics, I value the things I learned and still use the knowledge today.

Another extracurricular activity that I took part in was a musical operetta called *Down in the Valley*. I was in the choir and loved singing the songs. I was part of the alto section. It was great to be involved in that musical, and part of the Aden Bowman school choir.

When we moved to Saskatoon, we joined Third Avenue United Church, the church that Aunt Doree and Uncle Allister belonged to. Aunt Doree was a member of the choir, so she encouraged Merla, Karen and me to join as well. We loved singing in that big choir, and it was a wonderful chance to continue our music. Merla especially enjoyed it. She began taking singing lessons and developed her voice. She absolutely loved her years in Third Avenue Choir. She still takes a lesson every once in a while to keep up with her singing.

We became part of the Third Avenue Young People's group. We met several friends, and Cheryl Stacey became a very special one of mine. We were always together and shared an interest in sports. This was our social activity in Saskatoon. In the winter, the Young People's would play broom ball against other United Church Young People's in the city. Our cousin Val was part of St. Thomas Wesley Young People's. Saturday night we would have a broom ball game and then go back to the church for a study discussion, hot chocolate and lunch. Although I would often embarrass Merla by making some silly remark in the discussion, I often think of those times and the fun we had. Cheryl enjoyed embarrassing her sister Darlene also. The activities in the summer as part of Young People's were often swimming at Riversdale Pool or playing flag football in the park. Both boys and girls mixed. We enjoyed those fun times.

Chapter Nine

A Career

A
fter graduating from Aden Bowmen, I applied to Teachers' College on Avenue A in Saskatoon, now called Idylwyld Drive. I was accepted and started in the fall of 1962. My friend Maureen also attended Teachers' College. We would catch the bus and ride downtown, transfer at the old Eaton's store on Third Avenue and travel up Avenue A to the college, which later became known as Avenue A Campus of the university, and then the Saskatchewan Institute of Applied Science and Technology, and the polytechnic which it is a part of today. Maureen and I were put in the same class at Teachers' College. I enjoyed my year there, and due to my fun-loving attitude in school I managed to find opportunities to fool around and have fun as well. There were sports to get involved in, and I loved to play volleyball. I remember meeting a girl who was also very good in sports and on our volleyball team. All of a sudden, she stopped attending class and dropped off the team. I never saw her again, and I asked where she was and why she had stopped coming. She was a good student and an excellent athlete. I was told that she had decided to go into the convent

and become a nun. This really puzzled me. Why would she choose that life? She was always so much fun and such a good student and athlete. I couldn't understand her choice, and I often thought about her. Her decision to leave Teachers' College and enter the convent was something I often pondered.

In the summer after I graduated from Teachers' College, I applied to the University of Saskatchewan to take English 102, which I needed to get my standard teacher's certificate. My cousin Val also applied to take English 102. After obtaining my standard A certificate I applied for a teacher's position in Beechy, Saskatchewan. I was contacted and asked if I would accept a position in Strongfield, Saskatchewan instead.

Chapter Ten

My New Home

My dad loved the opportunity to drive to new parts of the province. He loved his vehicles and getting out on the road, but he was never too eager to let us drive his car. He suggested that we drive to Strongfield to have a look at the community. Strongfield is a very small village about an hour straight south of Saskatoon. We left Saskatoon and drove to Kenaston on Highway 11, then turned on Highway 15 and headed west. As we came to the crest of the hill a couple miles out of Kenaston, we looked at the road ahead. Dad never made too much conversation, but I remember him saying, "Whoever surveyed this road must have been drunk!" I think of his words every time I am driving home from Saskatoon. Highway 15 is a crooked road going west from Kenaston to Outlook. We turned south on Highway 19, going by the village of Hawarden. The next community is Strongfield, thirteen kilometres east of the Gardiner Dam.

As we drove into Strongfield, we saw it was a pretty little village with big poplar trees on each side of the main street, and a large cluster of trees at the end where the station house was located. There was a general store and café on the southwest corner of the first intersection, and the school was just kitty-corner from this café. On the corner of the schoolground stood a unique cenotaph. The site consists of a large steel sculpture of a soldier mounted on a steel base with memorial tablets affixed to it. The cenotaph occupies a prominent position along the roadway into the village. To this day you often see visitors come into the village to look at it.

Dad went into the store and asked about the community. Because of my interest in sports, I wanted to know if there was a rink in the community. We found out that they had just built a new curling centre at the north end of town. That sold me. At twenty years old I left home. I decided I would accept the teaching position in Strongfield.

This was the fall of 1963, when the Gardiner Dam was being built on the South Saskatchewan River. It is the largest embankment dam in Canada and one of the largest in the world. Many of my students were the children of families who lived west of Strongfield in the temporary community of Cutbank, and whose fathers worked on the construction of the river-dam project. Some of the construction workers also lived in Strongfield.

I found a boarding place with Bertha MacPherson and her two daughters just south of the café. I fit into the community immediately. I spent many hours at the school in the evenings preparing lessons. After supper I often played ball or catch with my landlady's daughters, and in the winter I curled at the local rink. Strongfield also had a hockey team, so I attended games at the rink and even played some women's hockey. One of my first purchases with my first paycheque was a new ball glove that I was very proud of. I also bought myself a new pair of skates. I had never had a pair of new skates, and these ones had good support so I was able to stand up straight and not go over on my ankles.

It wasn't long before I found out that Strongfield was a very musical community, and I was soon asked to join the choir in the local United Church. The community was a good fit for me, full of sports and music, the two things that I was interested in. I had found a new home.

Chapter Eleven

"You Have to Meet George Bristow"

W hen a new teacher came into a community, almost everyone thought they would stay there for good. I think the mission of anyone boarding a teacher was to marry them off to a local boy. The Strongfield community boasted many former teachers. My landlady was determined that I should meet a local farmer in town, George Bristow. He was an only child, and everyone thought he would be the perfect catch for a young teacher coming into the community. I wasn't the least bit interested in meeting George. I was interested in sports and enjoying events in the community, or being with teachers at the school and the nearby schools in Loreburn and Elbow.

I was walking home after school one afternoon when a big burgundy Imperial pulled up beside me and a tall handsome fellow asked if I would like a ride. I politely said, "No thank you, I just live right there," and I pointed to Bertha's house. When I told Bertha about this, she said, "Oh, that was George Bristow. You have to get to know him." It wasn't long before I got the opportunity again. George stopped me again when I was going home from working at the school. He asked me if I would like to go for a ride on the weekend, and this time I accepted. It was my first date with George Bristow. We drove to Saskatoon that night, and I had him pick up my girlfriend Cheryl to come along with us. He took us to the A&W on Eighth Street. We had a hamburger and a root beer. Not long after that trip, I got a letter from Cheryl. She said, "You have to hang on to that guy George! He is the first guy that ever bought us a hamburger AND a root beer!" George had made a hit with both Cheryl and me that night.

I did hang on to George, or he hung on to me! He was very persistent, and we went many places together: hockey games, sports days, drive-in theatres and movies. We had lots of fun together. We both loved sports, and I enjoyed being with his friends and cousins, whom he hung around with in Strongfield and area. There were Halloween escapades and parties. I was introduced to alcohol as a part of the parties. Although I thought I was having a lot of fun with my new friends, I always felt guilty about the free-flowing alcohol at the parties, and some of the young kids would get pretty inebriated. There were some times I would get a little tipsy, and I definitely felt guilty about that. Alcohol was never a part of our family. We never saw it in our house growing up, except at Christmas. Dad would have a friend or business associate from Searle Grain in for a drink, but it was *one* drink, then he would put the bottle away, up in the cupboard until the next Christmas. I felt that my parents would be really upset if they knew this was part of my social life. My dad's words would ring in my ear: "Don't do anything that would hurt your mom!" Also, Mom always said that a teacher is held in high respect in a community and should be a good example. Deep down in my conscience this lifestyle didn't make me feel right.

George and I dated for three years. I got to know his parents, and he took me to family gatherings. I learned to play the card games that his parents enjoyed. George also loved a good game of cards. Hearts was a favourite. I often remember seeing his dad's whole body shake with laughter, and I knew that he was about to stick me with the Queen of Spades.

In the fall of 1965, we went to Saskatoon to see my parents. As I was about to get out of the car, George said, "There is something for you in the glove compartment." I popped it open to find a small package within. I opened the package, and there sat a solitary diamond ring. I was excited and put it on and went in to show it to my family. They were all very happy for me. Mom and Dad liked George. They felt he was a responsible young man. Dad told George that night that he had raised me, and now George could look after me! George often remembers their conversation. We were young, only twenty-three years old. We went back to Strongfield and visited several friends, showing them my diamond ring. It was a night of celebration. Lastly, we went to show George's parents, who were already in bed. I think it may have been a shock to them, as his Mom said, "Oh, you foolish kids, it is time you were in bed!" Both his mom and dad were very happy; that was just a late-night response! They welcomed me and loved me as their daughter.

George's mother's sister had always lived up the street from him, less than a block away. Mildred and her husband, Allan, had three girls: twins, Jean and Joan, and a younger sister, Judy.

They were like sisters to George. Often when he finished lunch at home, he would go up the street and have more dessert at his Aunt Milly's. They had moved to Saskatoon the year I came to Strongfield, so we weren't with them as much when I was going out with George, but these girls always had many stories to tell about him growing up. He had always thought a lot of Jean, Joan and Judy. They were like sisters to George. We had to make a trip to Saskatoon to introduce me to their family.

Chapter Twelve

Wedding Plans

Each year after coming to Strongfield as a teacher, I had taken university classes during the summer holidays. Because of my interest in sports, I took physical education classes with plans to get my PE degree. I also drove to Saskatoon one evening a month throughout the year and took a class, first music then psychology.

After becoming engaged, I decided that I would not take a class the following summer and we would plan our wedding for July. We set the date of July 9, 1966 and started to make plans. George's mom and dad decided that it was time they retired, so they bought a house in Saskatoon and let George and me move into their house in Strongfield.

It was a busy year, teaching and making wedding plans. My pupils at school were very excited. They wanted to help me with wedding plans. The little girls made hundreds of tissue flowers throughout the year for decorating the cars and the hall. We would have our wedding at Third Avenue Church in Saskatoon, where our family attended, and the reception would also be in Saskatoon. We booked JD's restaurant on the outskirts of Saskatoon. The dance would be in Strongfield. My family decided that they would sew the dresses. Merla would sew my dress, and one for Karen and Vicki with Mom's help. I asked my girlfriend Cheryl along with Karen and Vicki to be my bridesmaids. Merla would sing, of course. I always wished afterwards that I had asked my cousin Val to be a bridesmaid also, but we had decided three would be enough. The style of the dress was a straight A-line shirt with a high empire waistline. Merla's would be the same, only hers wouldn't be a long dress, dropping instead just below her knees. That was her decision. She was delighted to plan much of my wedding. Merla and I went shopping for material. We thought that we picked the prettiest fabric, and decided that each bridesmaid would have a different pastel colour. Merla loved this sort of thing and was as excited as I was, maybe even more so.

George chose to have two cousins stand up with him, one from each side of his family, as well as a good friend, Dale Lemke. George and Dale Bristow farmed together, so Dale would be his best man. My brother, Kent, and Dean Norrish, a long-time friend of George's, would be ushers.

We had to take a marriage preparation class with the minister of the church, who at that time was a man named Rev. Wilmes. I'll never forget going to those classes. George and I sat on the chesterfield like two scared kids. Rev. Wilmes didn't do a lot of talking. I remember long periods of silence with this very reverent man looking at us. I felt that he looked right through us—God looking at us and pointing out the sin in our lives! I wondered if he would allow us to get married, or if he thought we weren't right for each other, or maybe too young?

My Aunt Doree loved to plan special events, and she and Mom, along with Merla, Karen and Vicki, planned the trousseau tea. Adell, Doree and Mom made special dainties. They hung up the bridesmaids' dresses for people to see. I had a couple of showers beforehand, one in Strongfield and one in Saskatoon. The gifts from the showers were displayed downstairs in our rumpus room for people to see. I remember getting seven teapots! I had never attended a shower like the one in Strongfield before. The whole community came and brought gifts. As the bride, I had to sit up front with my mother and soon-to-be mother-in-law. After the gifts were opened, they were passed around for everyone to look at. My past experiences with showers were in small houses where a few friends and relatives sat around the living room. My trousseau tea was more like this idea, but many friends from Strongfield came along with a few friends and cousins from Saskatoon. I was very self-conscious, probably acting foolish to cover it up!

The wedding day finally arrived on a very hot day. Like every young bride, I was extremely excited. I remember that I was so excited at the reception I could hardly eat. This wasn't very good, because when we got to Strongfield we had a few drinks before the dance. There wasn't alcohol at the wedding, but we had stopped at other places. I liked to dance and had spent many evenings at the school during the year teaching George. I had taken social dancing as part of one of my physical education classes. He had never complained about learning to dance, but later decided he didn't like it. It was the custom at about midnight for the bride and groom to change into going-away clothes and leave on their honeymoon. My going-away dress was turquoise with white lace over top. I wore white gloves and a white hat. We went to the Park Town Hotel bridal suite in Saskatoon.

After our wedding night in Saskatoon, we left on our honeymoon, a trip to Disneyland in Los Angeles. We drove through Yellowstone National Park and then on down through Nevada, where we stayed in a room in Cedar City that had a round bed. I had to send postcards back to my family telling them about the bed. Disneyland was very interesting, but by this time I was starting to miss home and my family and friends. We drove nonstop to Burnaby B.C., where we went to see my aunts and uncles, my mom's sisters. George still laughs about our nonstop trip to see some of my relatives. It was good to get home from B.C. and begin our married life at our home in Strongfield.

Soon after getting back to Strongfield, it was harvest time. George's mom educated me on making big meals to take to the field. The first meal I cooked for George was macaroni casserole. This was new to him, because his mom had always cooked meat and potatoes. Wieners were a no-no and so was bologna. I liked things like that! George's mom liked to come down from Saskatoon and help cook for harvest. We took full-course meals with pie for dessert, even a turkey dinner with all the trimmings.

My friend Cheryl came to help me one time, so George's mom stayed home. We made pumpkin pie for dessert and put the whipped cream on it while it was still warm. We set the pies on the chair, ready to go out the door to the field. The next time we looked at the pies the cream was on the floor. We used a spatula, scooped up the cream and put it back on the pies. We thought that with the dust they ate in the field they would never know the difference. Both Cheryl and I had a good laugh at our craftiness. This secret was never revealed to George's mom!

That first year of marriage, I used to love to ride in the tractor with George. When he was combining near town I would run out across the field, jumping over the swaths, and get into the combine to ride around with him. These combines did not have cabs; they were open-air. I would be filthy when I came in. I loved this new life as a farmer's wife.

George and me on our wedding day.

Chapter Thirteen

Welcome Donald Kent Bristow

I n the fall it was time to get back into the classroom. I enjoyed this time, and it was a short two-block walk to the school. George was still busy with harvest, and his dad was driving down from Saskatoon to drive the combine. His mom also came to get all the garden produce brought in and put up for the winter. She wanted to cook meals for harvest too. The schedule was planned for each family that was part of the Bristow farms. It was very important to George's mom that the men were well fed—none of them ever suffered too much! All the Bristow men were big fellows. They would crawl down off the tractors and climb out of the trucks to gather around the car that came to the field with the full-course harvest meal. George's mom would get a card table and chairs out of the car and set them up for the men, and they would sit down and wait for their meal to be set before them. It was a great family time gathered together in the field.

A few days before Christmas that year, I was visiting my family in Saskatoon. I was in the kitchen talking to Mom and thinking about how I would break the news to her that a baby was on the way. I wondered what she would think about becoming a grandma, and I was sort of shy about telling her. I finally blurted out that a baby was on the way. Mom said, "Dad suspected that a few weeks ago!" Dad was always very observant. My first pregnancy went well after experiencing some morning sickness in the first couple of months. George's parents were excited about their first grandchild also. I continued to be active during the winter months, participating in the local curling, taking part in ladies' bonspiels in the area. George's mother cautioned me about overdoing it, and she worried about my active lifestyle. By the end of the school year, I was looking very pregnant.

The summer of 1967 was the year of the opening of the Gardiner Dam. A big celebration with many dignitaries was scheduled for August. Diefenbaker was prime minister and would be in attendance for the opening. It was a very hot day in August. My sister Karen was working in one of the offices for the federal government at Cutbank and had many things to do in preparation for this celebration. Mom and Dad and George's mom and dad were down for the big opening. There were booths for food and drinks set up around the grounds, and most local farmers took time off from their harvest to attend the opening. I remember being very big at this time. My doctor even suggested that the baby might be early. This grand opening of the dam was a very hot, uncomfortable day.

On September 8 the men finished harvest, which was early that year. We went into Saskatoon on the ninth. We were at my parents' home. My family was all at home, and Merla had her boyfriend, Harold, over for the evening. We were visiting downstairs in Mom and Dad's rumpus room. It was always so nice and cool down there in the hot summer. George and I had planned to sleep at his parents' house, because there was more room there than at my family home. We left at about eleven to go to his parents' place. Just as we walked up the stairs and opened the door, I said to George, "My water broke." He said, "Oh no, it is just raining!" I looked at him and said, "Not where this came from!" We were quickly on our way to the hospital. At 2:00 p.m. the next afternoon, Sunday, September 10, after a hard labour, Donald Kent was born. He was named after George's dad and my brother, Kent. I remember him crying as I looked at him. Doctor Hindmarsh held him up for me to see, and then the nurse took him to clean up. I was exhausted. George soon joined me. It seemed like a long time before they brought my baby to be with me.

Doctor Hindmarsh came into my private room with Donald all wrapped up in blankets. He explained that my baby had a tiny harelip, but it could easily be repaired. He would get us in touch with a well-known plastic surgeon, Dr. Chasmar. As Donald lay beside me, I could see it was hardly even noticeable. He was a lovely-looking baby boy, with lots of dark hair like his dad.

The next day, George's cousin, Dale Bristow, was leaving for Expo in Montreal. He wanted to see our baby boy and the new mother. Dale was known for his pranks and getting a rise out of whomever he could. He managed to sneak up the back stairway and into my room. When he got on the maternity ward, he was asked whom he was there to see. He told the nurse that he was there to see me, and that he was the father of the baby! We all got a big laugh out of his story. Dale left with some friends and was off to Expo 67 in Montreal.

Five days later, I was discharged from the hospital. My family was waiting anxiously at Mom and Dad's. It was a hot September day, and I had poor Donald wrapped up snugly in a receiving blanket and a beautiful white crocheted afghan that had been given to me for our new baby. Merla rushed out to meet us as we drove up to the house at 1506 Isabella Street. She took my baby from me, and we all went into the house to admire this new member of our family. Poor Donald was covered in a heat rash from his warm blankets. He was passed around for everyone to hold. Indeed, he was very special: the first grandchild for Mom and the first nephew for Merla, Karen, Vicki and Kent. The next stop was at 57 Moxon Crescent. Grandma and Grandpa Bristow, George's parents, were very proud of their first grandchild. He received lots of gifts from both sides of the family and was a real delight to everyone.

I enjoyed being a new mother. Donald was a good baby. It was a delight to visit friends and show him off. We took him everywhere with us and had friends and family come and visit. I loved to dress him up in little outfits with matching socks. My favourite outfit was a little pair of sleepers like a ball uniform. He would be my little ball player!

Chapter Fourteen

Junior Choir
and Other Activities

Because of my interest in music, the congregation of Strongfield United Church soon had me involved with the choir and asked if I would lead a junior group. I had never led a choir before, but I certainly had lots of experience with them. I even decided, with Merla and Mom's encouragement, that I would take some singing lessons in Saskatoon. I hadn't gone back to teaching after Donald was born, so once a week I would drive into Saskatoon to attend singing lessons for an hour. My family was only too happy to keep Donald while I had the lesson.

After Christmas I started curling again. George was very good about looking after Donald, but it was usually for short periods of time. He wasn't fussy about changing diapers. After Donald was in bed at night, he would encourage me to visit friends or go curling.

In January, when Donald was just over four months old, we got the call from Doctor Chasmar's office that they would repair the small harelip. I was curling with some women in a bonspiel in Hanley at the time. I would go to the hospital, and then curl, and then go back to the hospital. After the surgery, they put splints on his arms and tied them to the side of the crib so he wouldn't touch his lip. It was hard to see him lying like that. I would hold him while I was there, and when I left they would fasten his arms back to the sides of the crib. He was such a good baby. He never fussed about this situation, but it was hard for me to see him restrained like that. Mothers weren't encouraged to stay at the hospital for long periods of time in those years. In fact, visits were often short. Fortunately, the hospital stay wasn't very long. The mouth heals fast, and we soon brought him home.

Just after Christmas, I found out I was pregnant with our second child. We would have two little ones very close together. I thought that would be very nice, and I was hoping it would be another little boy so they could play sports together. I imagined two little ball players!

Donald was now six months old. On March 10—my dad's birthday—we had Mom and Dad and George's mom and dad, along with two of my aunts and uncles from Saskatoon, come to church in Strongfield to have the baby baptized. In Strongfield, baptism was a big celebration, and the congregation was delighted to celebrate this occasion with us. Many friends brought gifts. We had a big dinner at our house afterwards and took pictures. Donald was a cute, happy baby, and everyone loved to hold him and fuss over him. George and I were living the life of a rural farm family, enjoying our friends and our baby, and not lacking in any area. I don't think we really thought about how blessed we were. Life was wonderful!

Chapter Fifteen

⊖∞∞⊖

A Bend in the Road

W hen we were growing up, Mom often made us new outfits for Easter. This Easter I was three months pregnant. Mom, Donald and I had been shopping in Saskatoon. The girls in our family loved to shop, like Mom. She always enjoyed seeing the new styles. I bought a nice new yellow suit for Easter Sunday, with black shoes and a black hat. Mom laughed at me as I tried on hats, having fun wearing everything from the ridiculous ones to the nice ones that suited me. I chose a black one, a jockey-style hat with a narrow brim, turned down at the front. It looked nice with the yellow suit.

On Easter Sunday, the choir was to be singing. I wanted to be at the church early, so George was going to bring Donald and come a little later. I grabbed my books and rushed out the door. Catching my heel on the door, I fell down the one step, but I jumped up quickly, brushed myself off and rushed off to church. I didn't really think much about the fall. I hadn't hurt myself.

This spring I was twenty-four, and would turn twenty-five in May. The weather during April was lovely. The men were in the field early that year. George had hired a young boy, Rick, who lived in town, to help him pick stones.

On April 20, Donald was just over seven months old. He was walking around furniture. I had been spotting a little that day and it concerned me, so I was lying on the chesterfield watching Donald walk around the coffee table. He was smiling and happy, a cute little boy. I had put a macaroni casserole in the oven, because George was bringing Rick in from the field for supper. When they finished, I told George that I thought maybe I should phone my doctor. Doctor Hindmarsh suggested I go straight to St. Paul's Hospital in Saskatoon.

It was a beautiful evening as we went out to get into the car. George put Donald in the front seat beside him and I crawled into the back seat so I could lie down. We waved to our friends, who were driving by on their way to a Saturday night dance that was on at the local hall. By the time we got to Highway 15 it was beginning to rain, and the next thing we knew it was snowing. Great big flakes were falling. It was a real snowstorm. George kept asking me if I was okay, but by the time we reached Hanley I was feeling pain. I wondered if it might be contractions, but I put that out of my mind. I thought I would be fine. The snow was coming down hard, in huge flakes. George was having a hard time seeing and the road was getting slippery. Every once in a while, I'd lift my head to see how we were doing. Donald was sound asleep, and George was driving as fast as he could in the terrible conditions. I felt the car slip and asked, "Are we going in the ditch?" The back wheels of the car caught on ice built up on the side of the road and we flipped onto our side and then back up.

The next that I remember was hearing Donald crying. I may have been knocked unconscious momentarily. I reached out to get to him, but I couldn't move. George stuck his head in the door and said, "I have a man and woman in another car here that are going to take Donald into the city, to St. Paul's Hospital." He said that he and I would ride with someone else. I couldn't move, so George and another man lifted me out of the car. It was a two-door, so it was hard to get me out. I had been hemorrhaging, so my pants were wet with blood. I had excruciating pain in my back. The wet snowflakes falling on my face gave me some relief. I passed out and then came to in another vehicle on the way to Saskatoon. I remember asking George if I was going to die. He hugged me and kept saying that I was going to be okay. I drifted out of this world again. I saw a green field and a hill by a lake. It was beautiful and so peaceful. I felt no pain. I wanted to leave and sit by the lake, but I heard George calling my name, "Mavis, dear, we're almost there." I could see him holding my head. I felt like I was looking down at him from somewhere. "We're almost at the hospital." I heard a siren and saw we were following a police car through the city to St. Paul's Hospital. Someone came out to the car. "Can she walk?" I heard them ask. I answered, "No, I've broken my back!"

When I got into the hospital, I remember them giving me a needle in my arm for pain. A kind nurse cut off my blood-stained pants. They were burgundy slacks, a pair that I really liked, but they were covered in blood. She was so kind. She cleaned me up and kept assuring me that they would look after me. There were lots of people rushing around. Dr. Hindmarsh's familiar, kind face was in and out of the room. I felt in safe hands. I was dragged back and forth on X-ray tables and then put to sleep while they did surgery.

The sun was bright Sunday morning when I awoke. The ground was white with new-fallen snow, which made the sun shine even brighter through the big south windows of St. Paul's Hospital. The nurses were all so cheerful, and they were discussing what a hard time they had getting to work in the snow. I thanked God for the beautiful sunshine. I prayed that I would be cheerful when my family came to visit. I was. I was thinking of Mom at that moment, afraid the accident would be hard on her. I also thought of George and my sisters and brother. I didn't want George to blame himself for going into the ditch.

Suddenly I thought of Donald. Where was he? Where was my baby boy? Dr. Hindmarsh entered the room, walked around to the right side of the bed and looked at me. I asked him where Donald was and if he was okay. Then I asked where George was. I thought that I had seen him earlier. I couldn't remember. Dr. Hindmarsh said that they had kept Donald in the hospital overnight. He said that he had been making noises with a tongue depressor in his mouth as they rolled him down the hall in a crib. "He looked pretty good to me," he said. "I'm afraid the news isn't as good for you. There were a couple of vertebrae fractured and the spinal cord was severed at the T-10 level. We did surgery last night and put a brace along the spine. That means you will probably never walk again." He went on to tell me about a woman who had lived most of her life in a wheelchair. I only half listened. I tuned him out. I didn't want to hear about a woman in a wheelchair. I was sure this couldn't happen to me. I knew that with hard work and determination I would walk again. I would never be in a wheelchair. I looked at him and said, "I'm going to walk again." He smiled and handed me a book to read. I never even looked at it.

A couple of nurses walked into the room. They said it was time to turn me onto my stomach. A huge frame that looked like a narrow canvas stretcher was put on top of me. They put my arms down at my side and buckled me in with belts, then flipped me onto my stomach. They fastened a couple of boards onto each side of the frame and moved my arms out beside me. I groaned. It hurt. They apologized. Another nurse came into the room with a needle on a tray. "This will help you rest for a while," she said.

Lunchtime rolled around quickly, and the nurses were soon around with apple juice, consommé soup and a jellied dessert. Clear fluids were on the menu that first day. I was looking straight down at the floor from the old-style hospital Stryker frame while they fastened a board underneath it, and they put my clear fluids on the tray with straws in the soup and juice to reach my mouth. They fed me the dessert. The prone position was starting to get uncomfortable, but they promised me that after lunch they would flip me onto my back and get me ready for visiting hours.

My thoughts went to Mom, Dad and George. I wanted to be cheerful when they came to visit. I was worrying about how this would affect them. It wasn't long before I saw Mom's face at the door. She walked in, reached out and took my hand. It was so good to see her! I was cheerful. I assured both her and George that I would be fine, and that it wouldn't be long before I was out of that place. George told me that he had taken Donald over to his mother's that morning, and that he was fine. I wished that I could have seen him but told myself that it wouldn't be long. Mom was teaching school, so they made plans for George's mom and dad to keep Donald during the week and he would go to my mom and dad's on the weekend. Mom said that Dad really wanted to come up also, but they thought it would be too much on the first day. "He'll be up tomorrow," she promised.

My dad, although always very firm, loved each of his children dearly. He constantly worried about each of us and never wanted any harm to come to us. He waited up for us, and often paced the floor until we were safely home. I knew in my heart that my accident was almost more than he could bear. He said it would be too much company that first day, but really he couldn't bring himself to come that day, nor the second, but he finally came.

George sat by my bed and didn't say much. He asked unimportant questions, like, "What did you have for lunch?" He wasn't the type of man to sit for very long. He soon got up and walked down the hall. George loved meeting people, and it didn't take him long before he met other patients and found out why they were in the hospital.

Mom fussed over me: brushed my hair, put moisturizing jelly on my lips and did all the little things to make me comfortable. Soon a nurse came with another shot for pain. They gave me a needle every four hours, which caused me to sleep much of the time away.

The first few days passed quickly. I slept a lot of the time, but I remember the Friday following the accident I was emotional the whole day, tears rolling down my face. It occurred to me that I had lost the baby that I was carrying at the time of the accident. I don't remember if anyone had made me aware of it, but on this particular day I knew that I had lost the baby I was carrying. I was feeling really bad. I had thought about having two children close together, and in my heart I thought that the baby was another little boy. That dream was now gone. A nurse came in the room and pulled the curtains around me, giving me time to deal with the hurt. I had many friends come for a visit, and everyone went home and shared how good I was, that I was cheerful and positive. A close friend came on a Friday when I was having such a bad day. She went home feeling so bad. She hadn't seen me the way others had described!

That was really the only bad day that I had. I pulled myself together and remained cheerful and positive. I received many cards and letters. People came to visit and brought flowers and all kinds of little gifts. George was kept busy putting cards up on the wall, until the whole area around my bed was covered with get-well cards.

It took a few days before my dad came to visit, but I remember him standing in the doorway for what seemed like a long time before coming in the room. He didn't say much, but I tried to be positive. My family—Merla, Karen, Vicki and Kent—came regularly. Merla worked in the city, but the rest of them were working away from Saskatoon: Vicki as a teacher in Wynyard, Karen for the federal government at Cutbank and Kent on the railway. Marge, my sister, offered to be my private nurse, but I was being well taken care of. It was a very difficult time for all my family. They knew the facts. They knew the prognosis that I would never walk again. They knew me as a tomboy: ball player, curler, football player, someone who liked to run, play catch, climb hills and enjoy the outdoors. Mom told me many months later that Merla sat on the floor and sobbed, saying, "Why didn't this happen to me? I do everything sitting down. I'm a secretary, I play the piano and sing, and that can be done sitting. Mavis was active, a teacher, an athlete, the mom of a seven-month-old baby! Why did this happen to her?" I realized that it was hard for each of them to come, and looking back I often said that it was easier to be the person on the Stryker frame than the loved one looking on.

Looking back from years later, I realized that I had the physical strength and the inner determination to cope with the disability. I was determined to be the best that I could be in the chair. It was a new sport. I wanted to roll faster, be stronger, transfer (move from bed to chair, or in and out of a vehicle) better than anyone else. My goal was to be the same active person in the chair that I had been before. I didn't want people to see me any differently. I would be the best that I could be.

Many friends came to visit me. My friend Cheryl, who had stood up with me at my wedding, brought her fiancé up to introduce him and tell me of their engagement. She was excited and, as always, full of joy and excitement. They stood and looked at me lying on the frame. Cheryl's joy and sense of humour was always something I enjoyed. I hoped I would be able to go to her wedding.

Chapter Sixteen

May 2, 1968: My Twenty-Fifth Birthday

I could hear a group of people coming down the hallway of the hospital singing Happy Birthday. They entered my room with a banner, balloons, cards and gifts. It was a party! My good friend Sylvia led the parade. Sylvia and I had become good friends a couple years after I came to Strongfield. She lived out in the country about four miles. She was newly married to a local farmer. I used to ride my bike out to her place for a visit. She was also a good ball player, and just about my age. We enjoyed many of the same things. Everyone liked Sylvia. She was a friend to everyone, and always the first to think of ways to cheer someone up, or to come alongside of someone who needed encouragement. She was quick to offer a helping hand, and volunteered at the local rink, the school track meets or anything else going on in the community. She knew just how to make everything fun and had a friendly way of teasing people. Sylvia brought me all kinds of little books that contained words of encouragement.

As I lay on the frame, the poems and short stories in many of these little books of friendship encouraged me and spoke to me of God's love, something I had always felt deep down but never really thought about.

One of the little books was *Let Not Your Heart Be Troubled,* a volume of poetry by Helen Steiner Rice. I read this little book many times. The poem that really spoke to me was "God Knows Best." I read it so many times that I had it pretty well memorized after my months in the hospital.

God Knows Best

Our Father knows what's best for us
So why should we complain,
We always want the sunshine,
But He knows there must be rain.

We love the sound of laughter,
Of merriment and cheer,
But our hearts would lose their tenderness
If we never shed a tear.

Our Father tests us often
With suffering and with sorrow.
He tests us not to punish us
But to help us meet tomorrow.

So whenever we are troubled
And everything goes wrong,
It's just God working in us
To make our spirit strong.

This little poem became a huge comfort to me, and I read it almost every day. Fortunately, I was never angry about the accident. I never blamed anyone, and I never blamed God. It was something that happened, and I was going to recover. That is what I believed. My family and friends supported me, loved me and were always there for me.

The staff in St. Paul's Hospital was also wonderful to me. I remember one nurse, Mrs. Thompson, who was on nights for the first while. When I would be awake in the night, she would turn me on to my stomach and sit on the floor. From there she would reach up and feed me ice cream treats and visit with me.

Chapter Seventeen

Other Visitors

I often smile when I think of the several members of the clergy who came to visit me. I was usually embarrassed and uncomfortable when ministers came to visit. Rev. Harry Manning was the minister from our church in Strongfield. He would come every week and sit with me. I liked talking with him, and when he would get ready to leave he would always pray with me. I kept one eye open, wondering if people were listening and what they thought. Being prayed for was a little embarrassing at that time. It did become easier, but I remember being very self-conscious about being the focus of the prayers. Rev. Ian MacRury from Third Ave. United Church in Saskatoon came, as well as Rev. Wilmes, who had married George and me. He stood at the door for a long time and just looked at me. I felt strange and uncomfortable. After he left, I commented to Mom, "He knows where my back is broken, because he looked right through me!" Mom, in her kind way, said, "Now, Mavis, he just cares." I was feeling like a kind of spectacle. There were others who came also. Looking back, I am thankful for all who came, cared and prayed for me. God was working in my life, but I didn't realize it at that time. I remained cheerful and never complained to the nurses. I know now that it was the Holy Spirit working in me. Sometimes the pain would get really bad, but I didn't ask for a painkiller. I had the silly idea that if I could bear the pain a little longer it would help me to heal faster, and I didn't want to be a nuisance. I trusted the staff and felt that they were doing what was best for me, so I never questioned them. I wanted everyone to like me and I didn't want to upset anyone.

Chapter Eighteen

Rehabilitation

At the end of May, I was told that I would be transferred to University Hospital, where I would begin rehabilitation. The top part of the frame was carried down the hall, with my chart on my stomach. The nurses on the ward all came to say goodbye and give their best wishes. Love radiated on many faces as they smiled at me, knowing I was ready for the next leg of this journey. I said that I would be back when I could walk down the hall. They all smiled and told me to come back to visit someday.

I was loaded into an ambulance for a bumpy ride across the city to University Hospital. There, I was set down on the floor in the hallway of the emergency ward. I was just on the top part of the frame, so I was only about a foot off the floor. I remember watching many pairs of legs hurrying by. Staff were busy attending to their jobs and others slowly strolled by, awaiting news of loved ones or friends. It seemed like I was in that hallway for a long time, many thoughts and questions racing through my mind.

Eventually I was taken to a room where they used a sheet to slide me onto a bed. I was afraid. I had never been moved, except to be rolled over strapped tightly to the frame. I thought, *What if my back breaks again?* The thought of being moved was terrifying. There was an unnecessary fear that the move would hurt. It was painless. The head nurse from the rehab ward was kind and understanding, and also very efficient. She welcomed me to fifth-floor rehab. I was placed in the room across from the nursing station. They raised my bed a little, and it was a strange feeling to have my head elevated. It made me feel a little dizzy. At supper, the tray on the table was pushed right in front of me. For the first time in over a month I had to attempt to feed myself.

The next morning, after I had breakfast and the nurse got me ready for the day, I was raised up a little in the bed. A doctor hurried into the room, his long white coat flowing out behind him. His hair seemed to fly as he cheerfully entered the room with the words, "Good morning, I'm Dr. Kirby." Soon, several other doctors with long white coats filed into the room and stood around the bed. Some had little rubber hammers. Some had long, sharp needles. They poked my foot and tapped my ankles and knees. They kept poking me all the way up my leg to my waist, where I started to be able to feel something. When they poked the bottom of my foot, my big toe moved. I thought this was a good sign, but I was soon to learn that it was a spasm. Soon, the doctors left the room and stood out in the hall. I couldn't hear what they were talking about, but I knew they were discussing my condition.

Dr. Kirby came back in to talk to me. He told me that the next day they would get me moving. I would be going downstairs where they would put me on a "tilt board." I really didn't know what that was, but I was anxious to get moving.

When George came to visit that night, I was excited to tell him that they were going to get me moving the next day. George was very faithful. He came almost every night. He would often bring me my favourite treat: a cola and a bag of onion and garlic potato chips.

The first night in University Hospital, Mom, Dad and several of my family and friends came to see me in my new surroundings. They were all encouraging me as I began the new steps to getting better. I reminded them all that I would walk again, and no one discouraged me from that hope and dream!

The next day I found out about the tilt board. I was determined to do everything to get better and think about going home. I was wheeled on a stretcher to the basement floor, where the rehab gym was situated. The floor was busy with people in wheelchairs, therapists rushing around and volunteers and porters who were bringing patients to the gym and back to their rooms. They used a sheet once again to transfer me onto another bed, where they strapped me around the board. There was a strap around my ankles, one just below my knees, one at my hips and one just under my arms. They told me to let them know if I was getting dizzy. They were going to raise my head up to see how vertical they could bring the board. They would continually ask me how I was feeling. I would say, "Fine! Fine! Fine!" I woke up soon after to find I had passed out. They had placed me back down and put cool cloths on my head. I learned that day I couldn't push myself quite as hard as I thought. That was my first day of rehabilitation.

As the days went by, I would be busy going to and from the gym. I enjoyed having things to do. They soon got me sitting up and learning to balance myself in a sitting position. When my back was sore, they would bring in tubs full of ice and, using towels, they would ice my back until it was numb, then get me to roll over and get myself back up. I was determined to be the best at each one of these activities. There was another patient, Ivan Marcette, who was injured at almost the same level as I was. Ivan and I would sit at each end of a mat and play catch with a soccer ball. This was right down my alley. I wanted to be better than Ivan, so I tried hard to always catch the ball and throw it as hard as I could at him. We both enjoyed this exercise. Our next level was using a medicine ball, which was bigger and very heavy, but it was more fun to have a greater challenge.

When George would come to visit in the evening, he soon began to ask what I had learned each day. There was a small gym on the fifth floor where the rehab patients' rooms were. George and I would go down to that room, and I was very proud to show him what I could do. When they first told me I was going to be in a chair, I was very angry. I thought that if they brought me a chair I would take a hammer and smash it to pieces. I did not want to ride in a wheelchair! I soon realized that it was the only way I would get around. I decided it would do for a time, but I would show them. I would walk!

It wasn't long before I was determined to roll the chair better than anyone else. I wanted to roll faster and turn on a dime. I practiced being very quick, and I also wanted to be good at getting in and out, from the bed to the chair and back. I was proud to show my whole family what I could do, and George was always my best fan, encouraging me to show everyone all the things I learned.

The ward aides on the fifth floor enjoyed interacting with the patients, and with the time spent in the hospital I got to know the nurses and staff very well. I still correspond with some of the girls to this day.

Doctor Kirby always encouraged me, and he praised me for everything I learned. He would come into the room in the mornings and say, "How's my prize patient today?" I was determined to show him the progress I was making also.

I never complained about things. I wanted to be liked and I wanted their approval. I trusted the staff with everything, and I never questioned why they did things. I felt they would do the best for me.

One day, when I was brought my breakfast, there was tea and not coffee on the tray. When the nurse came in, I commented that I had marked coffee on the menu, not tea. The nurse replied that it was not her job to get things for patients that they didn't receive on the tray, but she went out and brought me back coffee. When she handed it to me, tears rolled down my eyes and I said I was sorry. She was the kindest person to me after that, always doing her best to please me.

When the weather was nice, the therapist would take me outside. Rolling around outside was a little harder that indoors, and there were very few ramped areas at that time. One special time my therapist taught me how to get into a car. They had an old two-door outside that was up on blocks. I used a sliding board to transfer into the car, then I was taught to fold the chair, lift it up onto the door frame, reach behind my bucket seat and pull it into the back seat. This was a real thrill. I always loved driving, and they showed me that with hand controls I would learn how to drive again. They took a movie of me, showing how I got into the car and pulled my chair in behind. They didn't show the look on my face because apparently it was strained, and they thought it showed that it was quite a struggle! I did get very good at it. I eventually loved to get in the car and drive. It was such a wonderful feeling of freedom and independence, and a way that I was like everyone else. Pulling the wheelchair in behind and later lifting it into a side sliding door of a van became very easy, and I learned to do it without any struggle at all.

Chapter Nineteen

June 15: My Sister's Wedding

My twin sister, Merla, was planning to be married on June the fifteenth. I was supposed to stand up with her, but even though I was in the hospital, the staff assured me that I would be able to attend the wedding. I would be able to have a pass for that day to get out of the hospital and go to the wedding. Another thing I was very excited about was that I would get to see Donald, my baby boy, and hold him. It was very seldom that George brought him to the hospital. Children were not brought into the hospital very often, and George would have to ask for special permission to bring him in. George would always tell me how he was getting along. George's mom and dad kept him during the days of the week, and my mom and dad would take him on the weekends. Mom was teaching school, so she was unable to have him through the week. My sisters also helped look after him when they were free. I saw very little of him, and when I did, he would make strange and not come to me. He would turn away and reach for a familiar face. I was now a stranger in his life. I had to let him go and let others care for him, because I couldn't. George wasn't visiting as often now that I was receiving rehabilitation. Things were busy on the farm putting the seeding in the ground. He would go home and work on the farm during the week, so he went from coming every night to coming every few days, or if it rained. My family visited in the evenings, and I stayed busy during the mornings and afternoons by going to the gym. George's mom and dad loved Donald, and they took very good care of him. He was a bright spot in their lives. They would often take him down to Strongfield. They loved to show him off to the people at home.

A few days before Merla's wedding, it was discovered that there was a blood clot in my left leg, a condition called *phlebitis*. This was a setback that was very difficult at a trying time. My leg had to be elevated. Doctor Kirby came in to talk to me, and he told me that I would not be able to attend the wedding. The leg would have to be elevated and I would have to stay in bed. This was a blow to my whole family. We had all been looking forward to me getting out of the hospital for this occasion. The nurses encouraged Mom, Merla, Karen and Vicki to bring my dress for the wedding, and the staff would get me dressed up so the wedding party could come and have pictures taken with me. It was a bittersweet time. Merla and Harold and Karen and Vicki came to the hospital after the wedding ceremony. George also brought Donald, all dressed up for Auntie Merla's ceremony. The tears rolled down our faces, but we had our pictures taken and I held my baby. The nurses fussed over Donald, and of course all the aunts did also. It was a short visit, as everyone left for the wedding reception, and once again I was alone. Mom and Dad dropped in for a quick visit before visiting hours were over. Mom told me all about the lovely wedding.

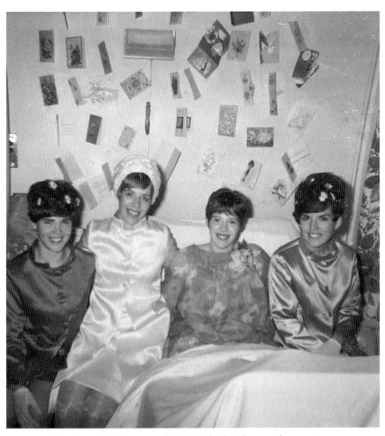

Merla with Karen and Vicki, the bridesmaids, coming
to visit me in the hospital on her wedding day.

Chapter Twenty

A New Way of Life:
So Many things to Learn!

I was soon to discover that there were several setbacks in the rehabilitation process, but I learned to accept each one. My attitude remained positive, and Doctor Kirby encouraged me by telling me that I would soon be back in rehab, learning to do things on my own.

Along with physical therapy rehabilitation, I went to occupational therapy, where they had a kitchen set up. I practiced doing some of the things that I would do at home. It wasn't too long before I was moved to another room on the rehab floor, where I had a regular bed instead of the hospital bed. I was expected to make my own bed and clean up my room the way I would at home. After a couple of weeks in this room, I was given a day pass so I could spend the day at my parents' home. We all looked forward to this day. Mom planned to have a barbecue in the back yard. She invited my aunts and uncles and cousins who lived in Saskatoon. Of course, George brought Donald to the hospital when they came to pick me up. We weren't used to using car seats for children then, so I held him on my lap.

What a joy to hold my baby. He never fussed, but when we got to Mom's he was anxious to go to her and then to my sisters. He was used to being passed around to each of them. He and I had to get to know each other again. My family encouraged him to come to me, and gradually he began to like sitting on my knee and riding in the chair.

Being at Mom's house certainly opened my eyes to the barriers I had to face in the chair. George helped me up the three steps into the house, but the bathroom door was a tight squeeze. I was able to get into Mom's bathroom, but when it came to going out the back for the barbecue, George had to help me out the front door and I had to roll around to the backyard. Everyone was willing to help, but I really wanted to do things on my own. Rolling on the grass was hard. The chair had narrow wheels, with smooth, solid-rubber tires that dug in. I had to get someone to reach my food and get things for Donald. My sister set his highchair beside me so that I could feed him.

When it came time to go back to the hospital, I was glad to go. I was able to do things on my own there. I rolled down the halls as fast as I could. I got in line at the cafeteria and was able to get my own food. I could easily get in and out of the bathroom, and with a transfer board I was able to get in and out of bed. I was independent to a certain extent, and it felt good! I could see that there was more that I had to learn before I would be able to go home. I wanted to walk again, and I was sure that I eventually would, but in the meantime I was determined to manage in the chair.

In occupational therapy I cooked in the kitchen. I ironed. I even did some carpentry work using a circular hand saw. I made a little table and two chairs for Donald to play at. I also made a rocking horse. These skills helped to strengthen my arms. I was getting stronger and more confident.

The day came for me to talk to the social worker about going home and how I would manage. I can still visualize her face as she talked to me, but I don't remember her name. She asked who would be going home with me, and I told her it would be George and Donald. She asked who I would get to help me around the house with Donald, and I replied, "No one!" She asked about my mother-in-law, and I told her I would be doing it on my own. She tried to convince me to get some help, but I was stubborn and determined to manage on my own.

Chapter Twenty-One

Homeward Bound

George was also anxious for us to come home. He was, and always has been, eager to help me in every way, but I was determined to do things on my own. He had prepared our home as much as possible so that I would be able to manage. Friends had helped him build a ramp to the front door. The door faced the west. The ramp had a landing at the doorway, then turned south and north, so that I could go north to the backyard or south to the road.

I had a ringer washing machine that George brought up and put in the front porch so that I could do the wash.

We drove home. We had an old-style children's car seat which certainly wouldn't meet the standards of today. Donald rode in the back seat. We pulled up next to the ramp at the south end of the house. I got into my wheelchair, then George put Donald on my lap and pushed me up the ramp and into the house. I looked around. This was my home, where I would have to manage with an eleven-month-old baby. Everything looked so high, the cupboards, the counters. I would have to work at the sink from the side. George and I didn't say very much.

Finally, he said that he was going to get the mail. He had hauled our things in from the car. The suitcases were on the bed and he put Donald's things in his room. I was left holding Donald on my lap and he was gone. That is what it would be like many, many times. George has always been very good to me, and he loves me dearly, but when he doesn't know what to do or say he suddenly disappears. I got Donald a drink of milk and gave him something to eat. He wasn't walking yet, but I managed to put him in his highchair. Then I put him in the crib. The tears rolled down my cheeks, and then I got mad! I would manage this home. I unpacked the suitcases and put things away. Some of them were awkward, but I got it done. I got food out of the fridge and decided on something for supper. The journey had begun, and I would be the mother and wife in this house.

Chapter Twenty-Two

Challenges, Frustration, Laughter and Success

As I adjusted to a new life, my community supported George and me in many ways. We had many visitors stop by. At first it was hard—not just for me, but for those who came to visit. It was hard for my friends to come at first, but after a few visits it got easier for them, and for me. At one time I said, "If you've come to feel sorry for me, don't. I want to be the same person I was before, and someday I will walk again." I told everyone I would walk again, and I believed I would.

I liked it when friends came for coffee, and we could sit and visit like before. My neighbour, Laurie, would bring her son, who was three years older than Donald, and they played together.

Soon I decided that I would roll over and visit Laurie, who lived just down the street with her husband, Dick. There was a seatbelt on the wheelchair, so I strapped Donald into it around my waist. We rolled down the ramp. As I rolled onto the road, I discovered the dirt at the bottom of the ramp was soft because of a little moisture. The little wheels on my chair sank into the soft dirt and we tipped over. We were still strapped to the chair. My neighbour across the street saw me and came rushing over to help. Donald was crying. She was an elderly woman, not even five feet tall. She offered to help me into the chair. I knew that would be next to impossible. I suggested she hold Donald when I got the seatbelt undone, then I proceeded to drag myself back up the ramp, pulling the chair along beside me. When I got myself up the ramp to where I was even with the height of my chair, I transferred across and into it. That would end my outdoor adventure for that day. It was also the last time I ever used a seatbelt in my wheelchair.

It wasn't too long before I ventured out again, and I made it over to Laurie's for coffee. There are many memories of times when I rolled over to Laurie's for visits. She would put a blanket on the steps, and I would lift myself up one step at a time and into the house. Then I would lift myself up onto a chair by using two others, and, lifting myself from the floor, I would slide onto one of them. We would sit and visit while our little boys played with toys. They especially loved playing with the big trucks and graders.

One evening, George and I went over to Dick and Laurie's to play cards. We took Donald in his car bed—a big rectangular vinyl basket that we could put the baby to sleep in. There were two handles to carry it. These were very popular for little ones in the late '60s and '70s. It was winter, so we bundled him up and George took him over, then came back and got me. After we had spent the evening we headed outside, George helping me home. There was lots of snow. George was running while pushing the chair, and we hit a snow ridge. I flew out of the chair and into a snowbank. Dick and Laurie were watching us out the window (we would later laugh about this many times). George got me to the house then went back and brought Donald home.

During the spring and summer months, George was busy in the field most days so I was on my own with Donald. Each day I grew a little more confident and would attempt more trips away from home. Eventually, I was able to visit other friends, and I went often. I would love to get into the car and drive, which gave me a real sense of independence. No one had a ramp, so I would transfer out of my chair and lift myself up the steps and into friends' houses, one step at a time. Eventually, some of my friends would pull me up the steps into their homes. Sylvia would sometimes get laughing and sit down on a step on the way up. There I was, balanced halfway, both of us laughing! I had a lot of faith in my friends, and none of them ever dropped me.

Going out to public functions was something that I didn't have a lot of courage to do at first. George, an extrovert, loved to go to activities in the community, so he always encouraged me. The first time I went to a public function was the retirement of my former school principal, Mr. Kyle. George's mom had come for a visit. I tried to talk George and his mother into going to the retirement party, but George was determined that I would go, because I taught with Mr. Kyle. I finally consented. Entering the hall full of people for the first time in a chair was extremely difficult. How I wanted to turn around and go back home, but he encouraged me, and soon he was visiting with people and I was forced to do the same. I didn't want people to push me around. I wanted to manage on my own, so I rolled over to a group of friends that I was comfortable with. I have always been thankful to George for encouraging me to get out and be a part of the community. It started that day.

Leading the junior choir was something that I enjoyed doing before the accident. It wasn't long before I felt that I could do it again. There wasn't a ramp into the church, so every Wednesday after school George would come in from the field to pull me up the steps and into the church so I could lead the choir. He would look after Donald for that hour, then go back to the field. He wanted me to do things in the community, and always encouraged me to be involved.

When harvest time came, George's mom and dad came to help with harvest. George's dad loved to be in the field. George's mom wanted to help with meals. I wanted to do it myself, but she was always there, planning a big meal to take to the field. The time eventually came when I took a meal out by myself. I hauled it to the car in boxes that I held on my lap as I rolled down the ramp, then put them in the trunk of the car. I put Donald in next, and off we went to the field. It felt good to be like other young women taking meals to their men at work. There were times when I had accidents and something would roll off my lap, but I would pick it up, clean it the best I could and off I would go. George's dad never complained about a little dirt. He said, "We always eat dirt in the field!"

Chapter Twenty-Three

More Rehabilitation

When I first came home from the hospital, I had an indwelling catheter for emptying my bladder. They had taught me how to manage my bowels by using pressure to release them. It seemed to work pretty well. I would try to empty them about the same time each day. There were times when I would have accidents, and this was a huge embarrassment for me. The physical part of rehabilitation was something I could control, but bowels were a different story altogether. I would just think I had it all figured out when things would change, and I would have to start trying a different approach. These were the struggles that often brought tears.

I have since learned that in later years paraplegics are not discharged until they have established a bowel plan. I was sent home to figure it out. I know now that I made mistakes and wasn't diligent about getting a plan in place. Managing my bowels has been one of the most difficult parts of being a paraplegic. There have been many tears when I have been alone cleaning up after an accident, putting my baby in the crib to keep him safe while I attended to the mess.

At the beginning of December, I was hospitalized again so that I could be bladder-trained and have the catheter taken out. Like learning bowel control, this was very hard. They removed the catheter and did everything to help me urinate. They would run water in the sink to see if it would help me—it didn't. I tried applying pressure, like I did for the bowels. Sometimes it would work and sometimes not. After much trial and error, and many tears and instances of incontinence, I finally seemed to be able to release by bending over with a sandbag pressed next to my bladder and pulling up on my feet. There was some incontinence, but most of the time I managed quite well. It was a wonderful accomplishment, because now I was able to get in and out of the tub and have a bath, which they didn't recommend I do too often with the catheter in. I would have to get a nurse to come and take it out and then put it back, or go to the hospital and have it taken out and go back later and have it put back in. Often, I would go to the hospital in Saskatoon, then go to Mom and Dad's, then back to the hospital to have it put back.

I managed emptying my bladder with the use of a sandbag for pressure for many years. It was about twenty years after my accident before they suggested an intermittent catheter, and that was because I wasn't emptying my bladder completely and there tended to be more infections. Infections were the most dangerous part of being paraplegic. There were not the antibiotics that are available now. An intermittent catheter was a huge advancement. I transferred on and off the toilet each time to put the catheter in and out. It was easier to use the catheter that way. Maybe the frequent transfers were good for circulation, also. I reused the catheters back when I started and

I reuse mine today, although there has been much advancement in types of catheters. At first I kept it in a saline solution. They sent me home with huge brown bottles of saline solution for cleaning the catheter. Eventually Dr. Kirby told me to use soap and water and keep the catheter dry. I still do that today and I have very few infections. I use one for a week before I throw it out and get a new one. If I am away from home and can't clean them I throw them out.

Chapter Twenty-Four

New Challenges

In the spring of 1969, a year after my accident, I decided I wanted to take a course that was offered by the Saskatchewan Teachers' Federation for teaching kindergarten. I stayed with Mom and Dad in Saskatoon and took the course, and Donald stayed with Mom and Dad while I did. In the fall I applied to teach kindergarten at the local school. At that time, kindergarten wasn't part of the school system for children's education, so I had to arrange it. I talked to the school division about teaching it, and to interested parents. I had ten children who would attend. There were six children from the Strongfield area, two from Hawarden and two from Cutbank, the community out at the dam west of Strongfield. That was the year that a man was put on the moon, and I remember teaching the alphabet using "A is for astronaut," and other space-related words. I enjoyed that year, and I felt so good about going back and managing the kindergarten class. A friend's little boy, Richie was in my kindergarten class. Richie often asked why I couldn't walk. The other children also asked why I couldn't walk. I explained it to them by using a lamp. I told them that when the lamp was plugged in the electricity travelled from the outlet through the lamp cord to light the lamp. If we unplug the cord the lamp goes out. Also if we cut the cord the lamp would go out. In the same way in our bodies the brain tells our legs to move. We have a cord from our brain down our back called the spinal cord. The spinal cord down my back got cut when I had an accident and my back was broken. Now the message from my brain to my legs can't get there, so I can't walk.

I would roll up the road to the school. The bathrooms weren't accessible, so I would make sure I could arrange my bathroom breaks at recess, or I would get someone to be with my class and quickly roll home, which was only a block away. George would take Donald with him. He would proudly stand up beside his dad on the front seat of the truck, wearing a little blue and white striped sweater, a matching toque, and a smile on his face!

I felt that I was showing people that I was the same person I was before the accident, and I was proving my independence. Actually, I needed to prove it to myself as much as I needed to prove it to others. I also felt like I was contributing to my community and earning a little money of my own, and it was something that I enjoyed doing. I felt good.

Kindergarten went every morning from 9:00 a.m. until 11:30, and then I would be home with Donald in the afternoons. Just before Christmas, I was having some trouble with bladder infections, so when I was done teaching kindergarten before Christmas, Doctor Kirby put me in the hospital to see if we could get the matter cleared up.

At this time, I had a feeling deep within that I might be pregnant. My period was late, but not that late. A lab technician came to take me for an X-ray. In all my experiences in the hospital, I had cooperated with everything they wanted to do, but this time I told the technician that I didn't want to go. This took a lot of courage for me. The head nurse then came to my room and asked why I wouldn't go for the X-ray. I told her I thought I might be pregnant. Dr. Kirby came to see me and said they would do some tests. After the tests, the head nurse came once again and told me they were negative, but I still refused to have the X-ray. Dr. Kirby said they would do the pregnancy test again in a week if I felt better about that. They did it the following week, and it came back positive. I thank God to this day for the courage to stand up for my own intuition, and for that feeling deep inside that I was indeed pregnant. I know God had spoken to my heart. As I look back, I see where God guided me at that time, supplying the courage I needed and the wisdom to be aware of my own deep inner feelings.

I finished out the year teaching kindergarten. Dr. Kirby arranged for me to see Dr. Frank Dyck, a gynecologist in Saskatoon. Dr. Dyck was wonderful to me, such a caring man. He hadn't had the experience of a patient who was a paraplegic. He arranged for me to go into the hospital ahead of my due date, because he didn't know if I would experience much labour pain. My due date was August first. Dr. Kirby kept telling me that the baby should be named after him. I would say, "I'm sorry, but it is going to be a girl." Two weeks before my due date, I was hospitalized. At the end of July, Dr. Dyck decided to induce labour. They had to stop, because the baby's heartbeat became irregular. The night of August first I went into labour, and a baby girl was born at nine o'clock in the morning. She had lots of dark hair that seemed to stick out in every direction. She was a good size, over eight pounds. I couldn't wait to take her home and show her off, but she became jaundiced, so we had to stay in the hospital longer than I thought. She wasn't a boy, but I still named her after the doctor who had always encouraged me through my rehabilitation. We named her Alana, after Dr. Alan Kirby.

Chapter Twenty-Five

Bringing a New Baby Home

After Alana was born, George was excited to go back to Strongfield and announce to everyone that he had a daughter. It was the long weekend in August, the date of the annual ball tournament. His parents were in Strongfield looking after Donald while he was in Saskatoon with me. He went up to the local sports ground. There was lots of excitement, because not only did we have the news of a baby, but another couple from Loreburn had had a baby boy the same day.

There was much excitement the day we brought our new little girl home from the hospital, and in the weeks ahead. Friends came to see our new little girl and brought gifts. I received dozens and dozens of cards from friends, and from people I didn't even know. Everyone who heard that I had a baby as a paraplegic was amazed. She was a good baby, and her big brother Donald, who would be three in September, loved to hold her.

There was only one thing that we didn't realize at first. When people came to see our new baby, Donald felt left out. He had always received so much attention, being the only grandchild of the Bristows: Grandma and Grandpa Bristow's "little man." He was also the only grandchild available for my parents, because my older siblings weren't around much. Merla had just had a baby in May, but they were in Calgary. Donald was always fussed over by everyone, and now this new baby was getting all the attention.

One day after company left, I couldn't find Donald. I called and searched through the house. I began to panic, wondering where he might have gone. I went out looking for him and found him out behind the house, sitting all alone in an old shed. He was feeling left out. I believe I scolded him for scaring and upsetting me, but after that I realized he was missing the attention that he had always had. He was such a good little boy, always doing things to please me. He was a wonderful help with Alana. He would go for diapers or other things that I needed, and loved to be my little helper.

Alana had colic as a newborn, but she soon outgrew it. She was a happy baby, finding her first two fingers as her soother early. It was a habit I couldn't break. Whenever she was tired, those two fingers were in her mouth. When she was about four months old, I started putting her in an exerciser that hung in our kitchen doorway. She was happy there, but every time I looked at her she was jumping on one foot. I would straighten her out, but she would soon be back to the one foot again. One day the public health nurse was around to see her, and I mentioned it. She put Alana on her stomach on the change table, and we saw that the creases at the back of her knees were uneven. The nurse thought it was congenital hip dysplasia or hip-socket dislocation, so she suggested I take her to the doctor. We were sent to a specialist, and that was indeed the diagnosis. Alana had to wear a plastic brace that held her hips in position and turned her legs out to each side. It never really slowed her down. As she grew older, she learned to crawl with the brace on and she also became quite a climber. I remember telling people how I once found her climbing up to the piano.

I always wanted her to play with dolls, remembering how my sisters and I loved ours. I got her nice baby dolls, but she was never that interested. She liked to keep up to her brother, always idolizing him. As she grew older, she loved to play games, especially board games. When she had friends over to play, they would love to get games out. We had many board games that Alana would drag out when a friend came over. Verna, a little girl from a few houses over on the next block, loved games like Alana. Alana had a lot of her dad in her—he always liked games.

Chapter Twenty-Six

My Little Helper

We had a general store two blocks from our house. It was so handy to be able to easily get bread and milk and other things that I needed. Although Grandma Bristow said Donald had talked at eight months once when she was looking after him, he never really talked until he was two. I would tape a note to his wagon, he would go up to the general store on the corner, take the note in to Leo or Dorothy, and come home with the groceries in his wagon. After Alana was born, this was something he did regularly. He grew up fast and became very responsible. He loved to do jobs for me.

Occasionally, during my pregnancy with Alana, I would be hospitalized to clear up a bladder infection or monitor my pregnancy, and then I would also have rehabilitation with physiotherapy or occupational therapy. During one of those times, the occupational therapist and I designed a table with a little cradle in it that would fit on the arms of my chair, so I could carry Alana around. This worked very well as I was working around the house. Donald would stand on the pedals of my chair and ride around, entertaining his little sister.

There were times when there were upsets also. One time when I went down the ramp with Alana in her little carrier (I may have been going too fast, I don't remember), the carrier went off the chair, and I did too. Fortunately, she was not hurt. Donald was right there to look after his little sister until I got back in the chair. Donald would at first like to push me, but I was always very independent and didn't want people to think I needed help, so I always discouraged George, Donald and the rest of my family from helping me. I wanted to push my chair myself, showing the world that I didn't need help.

During the summer months, George always played ball with the Strongfield Angels fastball team. I loved to put the children in the car and go to watch the games. I never lost my love for fastball. When George's parents were down, they loved to watch him play ball, so after we finished supper we would all go up to the sports ground if the Angels had a game. George's mom would rush around, asking people to move so I could get up close to see. I found this really annoying, because I didn't want any attention drawn to me. I never said anything to her, but I would always be very upset, and I'm sorry to admit that I would take out my frustrations with her on George. She was really only trying to help me and make things easier, but I did not want special attention.

Chapter Twenty-Seven

Trips to Saskatoon and My Helper

I often made trips into Saskatoon to visit my parents and George's mom and dad. They loved to see Donald and Alana, and it gave me a sense of independence and freedom to head into the city on my own. Mom and I would often go downtown shopping and take the children with us. Sometimes I would go on my own. There were times when I would look for a place to park next to an alley, because I would then get my chair out of the car from behind the driver's seat. I would get into the chair and be able to roll up onto the sidewalk near an alley. There were not wheelchair curves at the corners then. People would stare when they saw me put Alana on my lap, and Donald would hang on to the arm of my chair as we would set out down the street. We were not able to get into some stores, but there were lots of accessible places. Bathrooms were not accessible.

Children were always curious about my wheelchair. There were times when I would hear them ask their mother why I was in a wheelchair. The mother would say, "*Shush*," being

99

embarrassed about their child's questions. I always wanted to explain the situation, and if I got a chance, I would proceed to tell the mother it was okay.

> God will put his angels in charge of you to protect you wherever you go.
>
> – Psalm 91:11

Dad stood at the window with a scowl, a look I often saw on his face. One would wonder what he was upset about, but really it was a look of concern. I knew he was worried about me driving home with two little children in my car. Donald, Alana and I had had supper with Mom and Dad and were now heading home to Strongfield. It was a late spring evening in May 1971. There was lots of daylight left, but Mom and Dad would wait for my call to say that we were home. The kids were good in the car. Alana was in a little car seat in the back and Donald sat up beside me. He chatted away and asked questions about the tractors in the field. He knew his dad was out on a tractor.

I decided to take the shortcut just west of Hanley. That would get me home quicker than going by Kenaston and staying on the pavement. Dad would have told me to go by Kenaston, but he would never know. When I turned off onto the shortcut, there was a little muddy spot because there had been a shower. I went around it, stopped at the stop sign, then went up a little hill and down into a low spot. They never gravelled this road. Next was another muddy spot. I thought I could go around this one also, but as I began, we got stuck about halfway through. I tried to back up and then go forward. I was truly stuck! There were not cell phones back then, or CB radios. What would I do? I definitely couldn't get my chair out into the mud. George was in the field and he wouldn't miss us until he came home at dark. What if Mom and Dad phoned the house? They would be worried. I was annoyed at myself. *No wonder my dad wears a scowl on his face*, I thought. *I do the dumbest things!* There was a house up the hill about a quarter of a mile away, and I wondered if anyone might come along.

Donald was full of questions. "What are you going to do, Mommy?" I wondered if he could walk up to the farmhouse and get help. He was willing. "I'll go," he said. "I'll go and ask them to bring a tractor and pull us out." I pulled the hood of his little green jacket up over his head and did it up tightly. It had gotten cool in the evenings. I watched this little figure, not even five years old, walk up over the hill until he disappeared out of my sight. It seemed like forever that he was gone. All I could do was pray, and I did. All was quiet as Alana slept in the backseat. It was getting on to dusk. It felt like more than an hour, but I finally saw a tractor coming over the hill. The lights were on, and as it got closer I saw Donald sitting up beside the man behind the wheel. He had a big smile that I could see amongst the fur of his hood that encircled his little face. His brown eyes sparkled. He was so proud of himself. He had brought a man with a tractor. He brought help for his mommy.

Chapter Twenty-Eight

Stepping into More Challenges

Because of my love for softball, I volunteered to coach the local women's team. I loved the warm-ups, because I would get to play catch with one of the girls. They liked to throw it as hard as they could to see if I would catch it. If it was within my reach, I seldom missed. It made me feel so good to be able to get out with the women at a ball game and be a part of the team once again.

Afterwards, we would often go to the bar for social time and to talk over the game. We laughed at the times I'd become upset with the umpire about a bad call, or when my competitive spirit made me upset with the play of someone on the opposition. I'd holler at the opposing players, especially ones that were as competitive as I was. Along with the ball games were the social times with the girls, after which we would get together with our husbands, hire a babysitter and go out for the evening. An evening out would often be to the local bar. There were challenges there, because the bathrooms were not accessible. This would often mean that I would have to get down on the floor and slide into the bathroom stall, then lift myself up onto the toilet. If we could find an extra chair, I would set it in the doorway, transfer to it and then transfer again onto the toilet. All the transfers became less challenging as I became stronger and stronger. I prided myself in being able to do almost anything, and I didn't like to ask George for help.

One day, the school children were around selling big chocolate bars as a fundraiser. I bought a couple and left them on the table. When George came home, he put them up in a high cupboard out of my reach. I was furious! I transferred up onto the arm of my wheelchair sitting next to the cupboard, and from there I transferred up onto the cupboard, reached the chocolate bars and put them back on the table. When George came home, he noticed that the chocolate bars were down again and asked me who got them. I said, "I did, and don't ever put things out of my reach again!"

Grandpa Bristow spent a lot of time with us in Strongfield while he worked in the field during the summer fallow. George worked at the Gardiner Dam while it was being built, and later on the canals that had been built to carry water from the dam. Grandpa Bristow would often have golden corn syrup on a piece of bread for a snack. Donald would watch what Grandpa did. One day, he decided to have syrup on bread like Grandpa. I was in the bedroom tidying up, and Alana was just crawling at that time. When I came out to the kitchen, Donald had spilt the syrup. He was trying to clean it up, and Alana had crawled into it. I was cross at Donald for not asking me for help. I scolded him and sent him to his room. I put Alana in the tub and proceeded to clean her up. I had rolled in the syrup and gotten it all over my wheels, so I also had to clean myself up. Not only was the syrup on my wheels, but all over the floor too. I swear it was even in my armpits. I put Alana in the tub, then began to clean the chair and myself. After I got Alana out of the tub, I ended up getting in and washing my chair, not just once but several times. It was washed about seven times before I finally got it clean, then I fetched a pail of water and got down on the floor and cleaned it up, washing it several times. I was too proud to ask anyone for help, but I remember afterwards feeling bad about scolding Donald and making him stay in his room for such a long time. After such episodes he was always so good, and would try very hard to please me in every way.

Donald always wanted to help. One day he discovered I had taken hamburger out to have for supper. He put the hamburger in a pot of water on the stove, planning to make soup. In his enthusiasm he knocked the pot off the stove and onto the floor. Like previously, I came in and scolded him. Many times it was for fear of him being hurt, and this time my thought was that he could have burnt himself. There was greasy water all over the floor. I had a terrible time cleaning it up, because I was slipping and sliding all over. Fortunately, my friend Laurie came to the door and she helped me clean it all up. When we looked back at those incidents, we had many laughs. Picture a wheelchair in syrup, then picture it in grease, and remember those first chairs had solid rubber tires that were smooth! Not much fun at the time, but a good laugh later.

Chapter Twenty-Nine

Another Blessing

It was the summer of 1972, and I had turned twenty-nine in May. I was feeling good about many things. I seemed to be managing well in the chair. I enjoyed the summer attending the Angel's fastball games with George playing first base. It was fun to be with other mothers and their children watching fastball. I was also excited to share the news with the women that we were expecting once again. I felt that I was no different from other young women. Alana and Donald were good little ones. I was taking them out to visit with friends, and I was back leading the junior choir at church. Some of the women in the United Church Women were asking me to join, and I decided that I would like to meet with the other women. My first meeting was at the home of Betty Snustead, who played the organ at church. I liked to go to Betty's home and sing around the piano or organ when she played. She and her sister Isabel often played duets at church. They were a musical family, and I loved the opportunity to sing. Strongfield was a very musical community. Another friend, Carole Norrish, was also wonderful on the piano. She could make the piano rock! She was full of music. The women in the UCW would have wonderful programs and lots of music. We all had young children, so the little ones would have fun together when we would meet. Our UCW put on wonderful events, from teas to fowl suppers, and even great brunches. One time we blew the breakers in the church when we had electric grills and coffee pots plugged in for a brunch. Another time we had an international tea. About three or four women would work together on a certain country preparing food, making costumes and decorating a table to represent that country. Our UCW meetings were the main times that women from our church got together. We usually had devotions, a little program, sometimes singing and a great social time. At Christmas we would plan a special program and invite all the women from the community. After a service of worship, which included the Christmas story, we would go downstairs. We often handed out silly rewards for things. One example might be for a woman who had served a burnt meal to her family—we might give them a silly prize of some kind, a burnt potato or crust of bread. There was much laughter and fun. This would often be followed by a lovely supper. We did this for many years. Other events were valentine teas and bake sales. We would auction off items; pies especially would go very high. Certain people were known for cream pies with high meringue. Some ladies had a lot of fun trying to outbid each other for these pies, bidding as high as twenty-five dollars for one, which was a huge amount then, but we knew that it was a donation to the church.

Chapter Thirty

A Little Brother

When it came to the beginning of March, Dr. Dyck, my gynecologist, decided he would like to put me in the hospital, because he thought the baby was coming soon. I was there for over two weeks. On the sixteenth of March, I started experiencing a lot of back pain. The interns in the hospital kept checking to see if I was in labour. A nurse stayed with me most of the time through that day. She rubbed my back and felt for contractions. I was very uncomfortable and didn't even like having the nurse in the room. George wanted to be with me for the birth of the baby, but when nothing happened by midnight, the resident doctor suggested he go home and get some rest, because he didn't think there would be anything happening until morning.

I was left alone. I still had a great deal of back pain, but I was never someone to ring my bell and complain. I didn't like to bother the nurses. About 4:00 a.m., I went to grab a hold of my leg to turn myself over. When I reached down between my legs, I felt a fuzzy little head. The baby was there. I rang my bell. A South African nurse was on duty, and she came into the room.

When I told her that the baby was here, she knew just what to do because she had been a midwife in South Africa. She quickly had the baby lying on my stomach. She was wonderful. Dr. Dyck was contacted.

Then things started to go wrong . . . I started to hemorrhage. They quickly moved me into the delivery room. I remember drifting in and out of consciousness. Dr. Dyck came rushing into the room wearing a grey trench coat. "Get her legs out of the stirrups," I remember him saying. I hardly had any blood pressure and had to be given blood transfusions, but I was eventually stabilized and taken back to my room. George was there, and they brought the baby to us, a nine-pound eleven-ounce baby boy. What a thrilling moment! All along I was sure that the baby was a boy. We had talked about names and had decided on Cameron George. I don't know what name we would have chosen for a girl. We didn't have one, because I was sure it was a boy!

He had lots of dark hair, and we laughed at his big nose. He was born on St. Patrick's Day, so my dad thought he should have been called Patrick. There was a cousin of George's that thought he should be Patrick as well, and he nicknamed him Patrick. Cameron was the third grandchild for my parents in 1973. Two of my sisters had babies that year, Merla and Karen. They both had girls. After the trouble I had hemorrhaging after Cameron's birth, Dr. Dyck felt strongly that I should not have any more babies. He said, "Three children with a mother is better than four without." He recommended that I have my tubes tied. This was a very hard decision for me. I hated to say that this was the end of our family, but I took his advice and had a tubal ligation.

The day that Cameron and I were released from the hospital, George was busy getting me organized. He has always been a great organizer. He likes to plan things and know what we are going to do each day. This day he informed me that he had made an appointment for me to have my hair done. Now why in the world would he think it necessary for me to have my hair done the day I got out of the hospital with a new baby? Only George would think of that! We took Cameron to Mom to look after, and off we went to the hairdresser. He then proceeded to take me to the Canadian Paraplegic Association's annual meeting, telling me that Dr. Kirby said that it was important for me to attend. It was important for me to attend, because that year I was presented with the Paraplegic of the Year award and given a new wheelchair. This was a complete surprise to me. It was much lighter than my old Everest and Jennings that had solid rubber tires; this one had air-inflated tires with grips on them, which made it much easier to roll in grass or on the rough streets of Strongfield. I was delighted!

My sisters and I were anxious to get together to compare babies. It wasn't long before Merla and Karen came to see Mom and Dad in Saskatoon, and we saw that Cameron was the biggest of the three babies. It was thrilling to be together with all our children. Merla had two, this was Karen's first and I had three. Donald liked to be the big brother and cousin and hold the babies. Even Alana and Kurt, three years older, took their turns holding the little ones. Mom and Dad's home in Saskatoon became a busy place. Now that I'm a grandma, I realize it must have been hard on Mom and Dad having us all land at home with six little ones, especially Dad, who by this time was having trouble with his eyesight. Once in a while, he did take his turn holding one of the babies. Even though the commotion of having us all around was probably tiring, I know that they loved to have us visit, and they looked forward to having their family home.

FRANK DYCK, M.D.
F.R.C.S.(C), F.A.C.O.G.
RESIDENCE PHONE 652-1345

STANLEY J. VALNICEK, M.D.
F.R.C.S.(C)
RESIDENCE PHONE 373-3710

OBSTETRICIANS and GYNECOLOGISTS
321 MEDICAL ARTS BUILDING
23rd STREET AND SPADINA CRESCENT
SASKATOON, SASK.
S7K 3H3
Business Phone 653-5970

May 4, 1973.

Mrs. Mavis Bristow,
STRONGFIELD, Saskatchewan.

Dear Mrs. Bristow:

Thank you so much for the lovely card you left for me. You are a "saint among saints". Few people face life as courageously as you do - and most of us have no handicaps. In spite of your handicap you are always cheerful and I can't tell you how much this means to medical people.

It was a pleasure looking after you and I am very pleased that you now have three healthy children.

With best wishes.

Yours sincerely,

Frank Dyck.

Frank Dyck.

FD/rmg.

A letter I received after Cameron's birth.
Dr. Dyck was my gynecologist.

Chapter Thirty-One

Mother of Three

L ooking after new born babies was an experience I loved and I adjusted well to managing with my new born babies. I had a big table that I could roll right under for a change of diapers, or for dressing the baby. I kept things I needed within my reach on the table. I seemed to grow more confident with each of the children. When they were crawling there were more challenges. I found that the play pen was ideal if I needed to have them in a safe place while I went to the washroom or had to do something where I couldn't keep my eye on them. I liked dressing them in overalls or a little jump suit. I could then reach down from my chair and pick them up by the straps or the back of the jump suit. Years later I used the same trick for my grandchildren.

Like any young mother with three little ones, I was busy. Cameron was a good baby. He always had a smile. Alana and Donald were my little helpers who would get diapers for me and run things to the garbage. Donald would still make a trip to the corner grocery store if I needed groceries. When springtime came, George was busy in the field. Sometimes Donald would go with him and ride in the tractor while George did summer fallow. In those years, farmers sowed fifty-fifty. They seeded half their land and worked the other half. There wasn't continuous cropping. They never seeded any pulse crops in the area at that time either. Donald felt like a big boy and was happy to go off with his dad.

I was determined to teach him to play ball, so on nice spring days when we could be outside I would play catch with him. He would like to throw the ball at me to catch, and he soon learned to throw it straight to me, because if he didn't and I couldn't reach it he would have to chase it. Alana got interested in playing ball also, and would run after the ball and bring it to me. In our small village, there were all ages of children around. Donald usually played with children older than he was, but he was mature for his age and got along with the older boys around town.

In the spring George usually came in for meals, but if he was busy and wanted to finish up in a field, I would sometimes pack a lunch, and Donald, Alana, Cameron and I would go to where he was in the field and we would eat a picnic lunch. The kids liked it, but George wasn't much for picnics, so he liked to come home for meals. After the busy part of spring was done, George would be back playing ball with the Strongfield Angels. We all loved it when there was a ball game in town, because we would have an early supper and go to the sports ground. I would love to visit with other mothers, and the children enjoyed being with other kids. If George went with the other dads for a beer after the game, I would bring three dirty, tired kids home, bath them and get them to bed. I used to say that if there is reincarnation,

I wanted to come back as a man! But if George was around in the evening, he was always willing to stay with the kids and let me go to visit Laurie.

Many an evening, after I put the kids to bed, I would roll over to Laurie's. She would bring out her quilt and put it on her steps. I would lift myself up one step at a time into her kitchen, where I would lift myself onto a chair, and we would sit and drink coffee. I was always thankful that I never became a smoker, because Laurie smoked heavily. I tried it a few times, but never really liked it. We enjoyed good conversation, several cups of coffee and lots of laughs. Late in the evening, I would get down on the floor, drag myself out the door and down the steps, and into my chair. An elderly neighbour lady often watched out the window. We would laugh, wondering what she thought. Home I would go to my quiet and dark house and crawl into bed. After Laurie moved away, I often drove to Sylvia's where we did much the same thing, or she would come in and sit at my place after her boys were in bed. For friends' birthdays, we would often dream up some prank and go to a lot of work to decorate their homes when we could sneak around after dark. Sneaking was difficult for me, but I could often come up with the ideas and do a lot of the creative thinking and decorations. For Sylvia's fortieth, I made forty flowers and attached them to little stakes. Each stake had a silly saying on it referring to getting old, like, AFTER YOU'RE OVER THE HILL, YOU BEGIN TO PICK UP SPEED! Gerri, her husband Ross, George and I took them out after dark and pushed them into Sylvia's front lawn. The trouble was that it was October fifteenth. There had been a light frost. When we looked at our completed task, there were my wheel tracks all over the grass. Ross, Gerri and George were busy rubbing out the evidence of our visit. For my fortieth, Sylvia put a sign at the highway entering Strongfield: MAVIS' BIRTHDAY. COFFEE AT HER HOUSE SIX A.M. TO TWELVE MIDNIGHT!

Lynda and Ron Colton, teachers in the community, first lived across the alley, then across the street from us, eventually moving down to the end of the block, where they lived for many years. We watched each other's children grow up, and we became very good friends. We loved to spend time together, sharing stories, playing games or, on cold winter evenings, they would often bundle up and trudge through snowbanks to pool meals.

In the wintertime, I would be part of the program for ladies' bonspiels and dream up silly programs and skits with the other women for entertainment. I also made pies, buns, chili and many other things for the local bonspiels.

During summers, we loved to be at the ball diamond when George played with the Angels. George would leave right after supper and head up to the ball diamond to get ready for the game. He usually took Donald with him, because Donald was the bat boy. I would come later with Alana and Cameron, but when they got older they wanted to go with their dad. After I cleared up from supper, I would head to the diamond. One time, he took the children up with him and they went in the car, which had hand controls for me to drive. George thought I would roll up to the ball diamond. When I went out and saw that the car was gone, I was annoyed! I thought, *I'll show him,* so I got a baseball bat to operate the clutch, gas and brake, and got into his half-ton, standard truck, and drove up to the ball diamond. George was a little shocked when he saw me behind the wheel of his truck! After I discovered this trick, there were other times that I used his truck when the car wasn't available.

The Strongfield Angels usually had their annual fastball tournament the first weekend in August. Several women got together and made potato salad for the cold-plate supper sold at the booth on the sports grounds. Many teams entered, and it was always a wonderful day with people from all around the area coming to watch. They would set up long rows of tables in the curling rink next to the grounds to use for the supper. Grandma and Grandpa Bristow always loved to come for the tournament.

Chapter Thirty-Two

Fun Times Turned to

Fun Times Turned to Anxious Moments

The long weekend at the beginning of August was the date of the Strongfield fastball tournament. Everyone was up early and in a hurry to get to the ball diamond. Donald went early with George. I had to get some of my food ready to go, as well as Alana and Cameron. Alana was excited to go with Grandma and Grandpa Bristow. Grandpa Bristow's cousin Doreen and her husband Morley were visiting that weekend from Ontario. They all left, I got Cameron ready, and we went to the ball diamond. Grandma Bristow watched for me, and was busy instructing people to move so I could park right behind the diamond where George would be playing.

I hadn't been at the diamond very long when a friend came to me and told me that Donald, who was five years old at this time, had been running around in the rink with other boys and had run into the corner of a table and hurt himself. He was screaming with pain. People told me that I should take him up to the Outlook hospital to have him checked. Grandma said she would look after Alana and Cameron, and I took Donald and went to Outlook.

I saw the doctor in emergency. He thought that they should keep Donald in the hospital overnight to monitor him. I stayed with him for most of that day, and then after saying goodnight I went home. The next day, they discharged him, but that night he slept with George and me. He woke up about every ten minutes, screaming. At about eight the next morning, I convinced George to take him back to the hospital. I always felt guilty, because I was relieved when he and George left and I couldn't hear him crying. George came home about noon and I went up to Outlook. Grandma and Grandpa, Doreen and Morley had gone back to Saskatoon, so I asked a friend to look after Alana and Cameron while George went to the field.

I rolled into the hospital room to find Donald in a bed with a tube in his nose, having his stomach pumped out. The sight frightened me! I rolled out of the room, got in my car and went straight to the doctor's office. I said, "If you don't know how to treat him, would you hesitate to transfer him to Saskatoon?" Because Outlook was a small hospital, I wondered if he should be in Saskatoon. Maybe I also thought I would be closer to my parents and could stay nearby.

The next thing I knew, George and I were on our way to Saskatoon with Donald. He was transferred to the care of Dr. A. A. Dick, a children's specialist. I was sitting with him in emergency when the nurse and doctor came to put a tube back through his nose and into his stomach. They also put an intravenous drip into his arm. I almost passed out watching them treat my little boy. I always said that it is a lot easier to be the patient than to be the mother of a child who is the patient. Alana, Cameron and I stayed with my mom and dad in Saskatoon while Donald was in the hospital. George went home to work in the field. I was getting ready to return to the hospital the next morning when Dr. Dick phoned. He told me that Donald's condition was very serious. He had ruptured his pancreas, and there was just a thin layer of tissue over the area that prevented pancreatic juices from entering the bloodstream, which would kill him. He said that they would be keeping him in bed, very still, so as not to have it rupture. I was in shock as I got off the phone. I explained to Mom and said I had to go to the hospital. I don't know how I even got there. I remember that I even drove the wrong way on a one-way street. I finally got to Saskatoon City Hospital, parked, and pushed my chair out of the backseat of the two-door car. I got into my chair, rolled into the hospital and went up to the children's ward where Donald's room was. He had a nurse with him constantly, watching that he didn't move or get out of bed. My little boy was lying in bed, being very good. He was doing everything they told him to do. The nurse was playing a game with him. She looked shocked when I rolled into the room. She said to me that she had told Donald that she would watch for his mom to come if he told her what I looked like. He told her what his mom looked like, but he never mentioned the simplest way to positively identify me: that I would be in a wheelchair. I had always wanted to be thought of the same as any other mom, and I had accomplished this with my own son. I was his mom and the same as any other mom. He never saw the wheelchair!

Donald was in the hospital for over a month. I bought him a teddy bear to be his companion when I would leave him in the evening and go back to Mom's. We played games, drew pictures and read many books. George, who loved to play cards, taught him several card games, and so did Grandma and Grandpa Bristow. George even tried to teach him cribbage, and he was only five years old! One of the books I read over and over was about Pooh Bear. As Donald held on to his bear, I read the poem "Us Two" by A. A. Milne over and over until both Donald and I had memorized the last verse. The poem was about a bear that was a constant companion. In the last verse, the author talks about the boy who always kept his bear with him. He was his closest friend.

Donald turned six years old when he was in the hospital and would have started school that September. He got home in early October and I took him to school to begin Grade 1. He was very thin, but the doctor said that he would be fine now. I felt he should continue to be careful, but he was soon running and playing with the other children.

This wasn't the only time that Donald suffered a serious accident. It seemed like our involvement at ball games placed Donald in the environment where he was most likely to experience accidents. George's fastball team was playing in a tournament in Outlook when Donald was eight years old. He was the bat boy for the team, and he loved being with his dad at ballgames. He was very gung-ho, right in with the men taking part. At this particular time, he was hurrying to pick up one of the bats and got too close to one of the players warming up. He was swinging a heavy warmup bat, and hit Donald right in the mouth, knocking out four of his permanent top teeth. I was sitting in our vehicle with our other two children and just turned my head to see it happen. George and I rushed him to the hospital in Outlook, and then into Saskatoon to see George's cousin, who was a dentist. He referred him to an orthodontist. For several years Donald was without his front teeth. When he turned fourteen, the orthodontist used braces to move his back teeth forward until his eyeteeth became his two front teeth, then they put implants in the back teeth. Poor Donald suffered a lot with the braces each time they tightened them. He also had to have stitches in his top lip. The orthodontist and the doctor did a wonderful job. Seeing him as an adult, one would never know about this terrible accident.

Chapter Thirty-Three

Raising a Family

As our children grew and interacted with other kids, we wanted them to experience fun times like the others. In the summer, many of our friends went camping. We decided we would buy a tent and take the kids on family holidays to some of the parks in the area. We went with some good friends, Ross and Gerri Vollmer, a family that had children about the same age as ours. Camping wasn't the easiest thing for me, because back in the '70s and early '80s there weren't accessible washrooms in the campgrounds. We found a large tent with two sections. We put our sleeping bags in the section that had a floor. I would get down out of my chair and drag myself into a sleeping bag on the ground. The other part of the tent didn't have a floor, so we had a little folding table and chairs that we could put there if it wasn't nice weather. George also built a commode out of plywood for me to go to the bathroom. In the morning he would carry the "honey pail" to the bathroom and empty it.

When we pulled into a campground, the kids would love to jump out of the truck and run to the wood pile to get fuel for a campfire. They were so excited about setting up the tent. This was not the kind of holiday George enjoyed. Picnics and camping were never a part of his experiences growing up. During harvest times they ate meals in the field, and those were all the picnics he wanted to have.

For several summers, we took the kids camping and roughed it for their sake. We were all excited one year when George decided we would get a trailer that we could pull behind the truck. It wasn't accessible, but he built a little stool with castors on the bottom, then covered it with carpet. We kept it at the door of the trailer. I would transfer in the door and onto the stool and drag myself around the camper. I could lift myself up onto the bench at the table. He also made a higher stool so I could pull myself over to the stove if I needed to cook inside, and I could also pull myself into the washroom at the back of the trailer. There was even a tub that I could get into if I had to because of an accident with my bowels. When we were away from home and my routine changed, this is something that would happen every once in a while.

There were several summers that friends encouraged me to attend the Elbow Lutheran Bible Camp. George would take the trailer down and park it at the camp, and I would take the children and stay for the week. At first, many of the trails through the camp were pretty rough, but after I had attended for a few years they gradually got cement sidewalks all through the camp.

I took my turn helping out in the kitchen. I enjoyed the wonderful studies they had for adults in the chapel during the morning, and sometimes I would sing a duet with a friend, and even a solo once in a while. People always made me feel so welcome and appreciated my contributions.

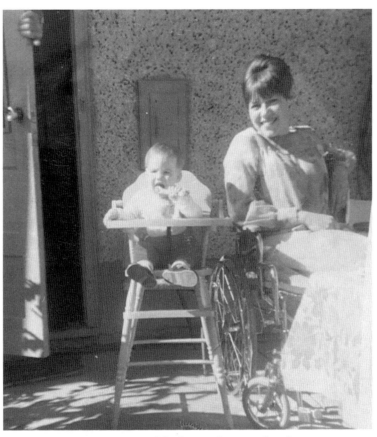

Day pass out of the hospital to visit family.

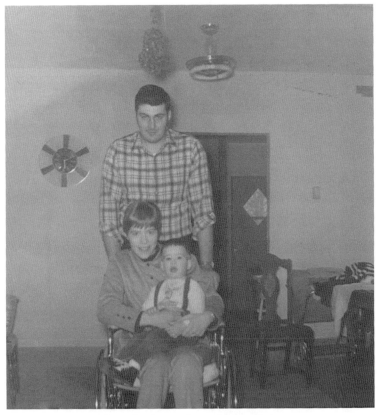

First day home from the hospital.

First baby born in Saskatchewan to a paraplegic, Alana.
We constructed that changing table at Occupational
Therapy at Royal University Hospital.

Our family in 1974.

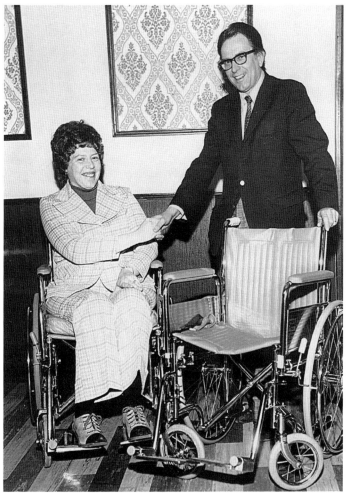

Dr. Kirby presenting me Paraplegic of the Year, 1974.

Chapter Thirty-Four

A Special Christmas Gift

The kids were up early to see their Christmas gifts. As had been our family custom when we grew up, I liked the kids to get dressed and have breakfast before we opened the gifts under the tree. They got a chance to open their Santa gifts and play with them, then we all got dressed, had breakfast, cleaned up, and then opened gifts from other family and friends that were wrapped under the tree. There was lots of grumbling, because everyone was excited to open gifts. George was disgusted with me for making this rule. I liked it, because after the gifts were opened I could start preparing the turkey for Christmas dinner. This Christmas Day turned out differently, because George didn't have a gift under the tree for me. He always had a gift for me, so I thought something was up. He told me to look out the window to find my gift. There, parked out underneath the window, was a new snowmobile. George had straps put on to hold my feet. I was really excited. We all got on warm winter clothes to go out and ride on the snowmobile. Donald was excited also. He was old enough to ride on the snowmobile, but as soon as we started it up, Cameron was scared. It took him a while to warm up to it, but Alana was gung-ho right away. We had a fun day on the snowmobile. We tied a toboggan behind it and pulled the kids in the field across the road from our house. George was content to let Alana, Donald and me enjoy the snowmobile while he stayed in the house with Cameron. He didn't want any part of this noisy machine. After I had been out for quite a while, I felt I had better come in. I couldn't feel how cold my feet might be getting, and I didn't want to take a chance of freezing them.

That winter, and many winters following, we had many hours of winter fun on the snowmobile. A group of women with their own snowmobiles often got together with me, and we would ride together. We had great times sailing across the fresh white snow, and then we would take the time to stop at a friend's for coffee. At some places, I would have to lift myself up a step at a time and drag myself in and up onto a chair, where we would have coffee and laugh about our fun. There were times when I would have to use a washroom, so, as some of the farmhouses were two storeys, I would drag myself up a flight of stairs and across the floor and into the bathroom, then drag myself back down the stairs.

During one ride, I hit a ditch of soft white snow. I was buried, but my friends pulled me out so that I could get back on the snowmobile. We still laugh when we get together and share memories of our excursions! Those were the days when I didn't have fear. I didn't think of things that could happen back then.

Chapter Thirty-Five

George and Municipal Government, and My Life-Changing Experience

In the fall of 1968, the year of my accident, some of the councillors and the mayor of our village came to meet with George to persuade him to run for the village council. He became a member of the village council that year, a position that would become a very important part of his life for many years to come. He served a short time as councillor and then became mayor, a position that he held for nearly forty years. This was something that he was very dedicated to, and, as it turned out, influenced both of our lives.

George had always lived in the little village of Strongfield, and he was proud of it. He worked very hard to keep it looking nice, and to see that there was progress and improvement to infrastructure and public buildings in the community. Not too long after going on council, he found out about a provincial program to receive funding to oil the streets in town. He and the other councillors felt that this would be more beneficial than spending tax dollars on sidewalks. Six years after I was confined to a wheelchair, another local resident was in an accident and confined to a wheelchair also. Bob Norrish was paralyzed at almost the same level as I was. Now that there were two people in this small village who used a wheelchair, the community suddenly became very conscious about making buildings accessible and making it easy for the two of us to be independent. The oiled streets made it easy to get around. George made sure that they were kept up every year. He developed a wonderful working relationship with the Department of Highways. They saw that the holes were filled and sand-sealed, keeping the streets in Strongfield in excellent condition. He even talked me into making pies, and he would invite the men working on the highway in for coffee and pie and ask them to sand-seal the roads in town that had cracks or holes.

After Bob was hurt, the community held work bees to put ramps into public buildings. There was one put into our local church. The community rink was ramped inside and out, making it possible for us to get into the kitchen, the dressing room, and out to the ice surface in the rink, so we were able to watch hockey or skating. Some of the local men even designed an electric lift with cables that would take us to the second floor so we could watch curling. A ramp and accessible washrooms were put into the local community hall. Many local residents also constructed ramps into their homes so we could come and visit. The community was very conscious of accessibility.

In the late '70s, someone from our church board found out about a lift that would go down over a flight of stairs. There were chains on each side of a platform that sat at the bottom of the flight of stairs into the basement, with controls at the top and bottom. The platform remained at the bottom of the stairs, and you could press the control and bring it up and then ride down. The church board, which George was involved with along with his cousin, Bob, got a company from Regina to install this lift in the church so that Bob Norrish and I could attend functions in the basement. It was useful for others who had a difficult time going up and down the long flight of stairs too. When I was involved with the choir, I often went over to the church to look through music for us. Often, I would go over by myself later in the evening and down to the basement on this lift. In later years, after 2000, our church building was inspected by a government inspector and the lift was condemned. I believe we still used it until the church closed in 2010. It was crucial to have access to the basement of the church for many functions.

As a member of the village council, George began attending the Saskatchewan Urban Municipalities Convention (SUMA) each year. He always encouraged me to attend these conventions with him. He was very proud of me and my independence. He liked to have his wife with him at the convention. The SUMA organization began to make their ladies' programs, and eventually spouses' programs, accommodating to me in the wheelchair. George ran for a position on SUMA and became the representative for villages in the southwest part of the province. Eventually, he was elected vice president for villages. It was a position that helped him to understand municipal government, and to be educated in many ways that helped benefit our own small village. It was also a very good education for him.

One year, the province was twinned with the country of Zimbabwe. George and two other men from SUMA, the vice-president of towns and the executive director, travelled to Zimbabwe. It was a trip he will never forget. A year later, three men from Zimbabwe came to Saskatchewan and George helped to show them around our province. He brought them to Strongfield and took them to see his farm, where he worked with his cousin and his cousin's sons. He took them on the big machinery and then brought them to the house for a supper of Canadian food, consisting of roast beef, potatoes and gravy, a vegetable and, of course, homemade apple pie for dessert that I had prepared. It was a special day for them and a special day for George, who always delighted in being a generous host. He also wanted to show that his wife was an independent woman and a good cook. At least he told people I was a good cook!

George and I attended SUMA conventions together for many years. I was always welcomed, and the executive went to great lengths to make things as accessible as possible. The first years attending the conventions did, however, bring challenges. The hotel rooms were not accessible. I could not get through the narrow bathroom doorways. We would get an extra chair or a bench, and I would transfer from my chair to another chair and onto the toilet, or into the tub. Fortunately, when I was young I had developed strong arms and upper body strength. I could lift myself down into the tub and then lift myself up.

I remember also that the public washroom stalls were not accessible. I would get down onto the floor, even with my dressy outfits, and drag myself into the bathroom and then lift myself up onto the toilet. It was hard and strenuous activity, but I was determined to attend the conventions as George's wife, and he always wanted me along. He was proud of me, and proud of everything I was able to do. I was determined to be as independent as possible.

The end of January 1983 rolled around, and it was time again for the annual SUMA convention. Our children were older, but not old enough to be left home alone. We asked some friends who lived in the country if they would like to come to town and stay in our house with our children for the few days we were away at the convention. Because George was on the executive of SUMA as vice-president of villages, he went to Regina two days ahead of me. We arranged that I would go to Regina with George's cousin Dale and another councillor from Loreburn, who were coming to the convention as well.

The trip to Regina was always eventful when Dale was along. He was always thinking of something to get people laughing. There was also a bottle passed around in the vehicle, so everyone was feeling happy and also kind of silly. We went by way of Moose Jaw, and when we stopped at an A&W for a snack and a bathroom break, Dale came out with a gift for the occupants of the vehicle—the toilet seat from the washroom! Only Dale would do something that silly. When I think of it now, it's clear it was actually vandalism, but he did it for a laugh.

When we got to Regina, we went to our rooms. George was waiting for me to go with him to the hospitality room where the rest of the board members and some convention guests were getting together. The president of SUMA that year was Mayor Herb Taylor from Moose Jaw. Herb was an Anglican priest, and so was his wife, Ruth. They were a lovely couple, and we enjoyed being with them. While we were visiting in the room, in walked Dale with a lovely bouquet of flowers and presented them to Ruth. We were to find out later that he had taken them from the hotel lobby! Even though I laughed about these escapades, I used to feel guilty about them, because I knew deep down they were wrong. I just went along with the fun and the laughter. Ruth was wise to his antics, and had the flowers sent back down to the lobby.

The next morning, I got up and, after getting dressed, I went into the hospitality room, which was joined to the room George and I were in. George was often in charge of looking after this room. I thought I would get a drink of orange juice or something that we had in the fridge there. Ruth Taylor happened to come into the room at that point, and we started visiting. Ruth was always a very gracious woman, and very friendly. She asked me about our Christmas programs, because she knew that I was involved with the children's choir in the United Church in Strongfield. I told her it went well, but we got talking about the lack of commitment of many people, and I expressed frustration about many who didn't come to practices and then showed up for the final performance and didn't know their parts. Ruth calmly said, "Why don't you pray about it?" I laughed and replied with something like, "Oh, I don't think God hears my prayers, or maybe I don't know how to pray!" Ruth said, "Why don't you come to my room later? I'll teach you." I was blown away by this statement.

When I went back to my room, I thought a lot about what Ruth had said. Part of me was curious, and part of me wondered what she knew—was there a certain way to pray? No one had ever taught us a particular way to pray when we were going to church, Sunday school or young people's groups. We were taught bedtime prayers or table grace. Many of my prayers were asking God to help me pass exams or something, or prayers after I was hurt, or worried about my children, and I really didn't think about the answers. I took them for granted, I guess. People offered to pray for me at the time of my accident, but I never really considered the answers. Why would I pray about the children's choir? Ruth puzzled me, and yet I was curious. After lunch I decided I would go and see her. I rolled down the hall and tapped lightly on her door. If she didn't answer, I was just going to slip away and forget about it. She answered and invited me in.

She sat on the end of the bed and we visited. She asked me about my family, and then asked about my accident and time in the hospital. We talked a bit about my church. Then she got up and said, "I'd like to pray for you." She walked around behind me and put her hands on my shoulders. She prayed—for me, for George, for our family, and then she prayed words that I didn't understand. It was just garble to me, but I felt warm all over, like I was sitting in a warm shower. Then she picked up some books and gave them to me to read.

I left her room anxious to read the books. One was *Reading Scripture as the Word of God* by George Martin. Another was *The Healing Light* by Agnes Sanford. Another was *The Prayer that Heals* by Francis McNutt. When I went home from that convention, I couldn't stop reading those books. They told stories about people who had been healed when they were prayed for. Could I possibly be healed?

The experience caused a hunger in me that made me want to read the Bible and find out more about it. I knew there was a group of young women who got together for Bible studies in the Strongfield area. They had invited me, but I was always too busy to go, or maybe just felt insecure about it. I found excuses not to go. I worked up the courage now and started going, but was embarrassed to let on how little I knew about the Bible. I faked as much as I could! I probably never fooled too many people.

The Lutheran church in our area was always very active. Many of my friends were Lutheran. They had a lot of Bible studies in their church that several of my friends attended. The next fall they were offering a study called "Crossways." It was an overview of the whole Bible. I decided I would attend the study with my friends. I did feel a little out of place, since it wasn't my church, but everyone was very welcoming and seemed pleased that I had come. I learned many stories from the Bible that I had never heard of in church or Sunday school. I learned about the good and bad kings in Israel and Judah. I learned about the major and minor prophets, and many other things about the Bible. Rev. Ken Wilston was the pastor at that time, and he was very encouraging and always willing to help me up the steps and into the church when my friends were pulling me in. The Lutheran church did not have a ramp until several years later. It was me who was the inspiration for them getting one, because I attended many of their women's programs and Bible studies. Since attending some of the Lutheran Bible studies, I have always felt that they were very good.

I mentioned previously about attending the Lutheran Bible Camp. This became a practice for many years around the first week of July. I learned so much about the Bible during those teachings at camp, from listening to the discussions. I often wished that I was good at asking questions, but I never did. I had questions, but was too unsure to ask them, often not knowing how to phrase the question! I just listened. I also enjoyed the music at camp, and once in a while I was asked to sing, by myself or with my friends Gerri or Marilyn. Marilyn was a regular participant at the Wednesday morning Bible studies held in Strongfield. These things made me feel accepted and valued. Also, I felt my Lutheran friends encouraged me to come when they made things so accessible.

I continued to thirst for more knowledge about my faith. One day a pamphlet came in the mail from Prairie Christian Training Centre (PCTC) at Fort Qu'Appelle. It was an event called "The Spiritual Path," with facilitators Gordon and Mary Tooms. I decided I wanted to go to this event because it was held in a United Church learning centre, my own denomination. It was a risk to venture somewhere by myself away from home. I didn't know how accessible it would be. When I phoned about registration, I was told they thought I could manage with some help. I decided I would go and find out. It wasn't wonderful, but I was able to manage for the weekend. PCTC was built on a hill. I could get down to the lower level by rolling down the hill and entering through doors on the basement level. The dorms had wide enough doors to get through. I was able to manage in the bathroom. I managed the steep hill with help from whoever was available. With my strong upper body, I was able to lift myself off the toilet, which was quite low, and I was able to lift myself in and out of the bathtub.

It was a rewarding experience, and one that ignited my faith even more. Three or four of the books that they talked about were ones that Ruth Taylor had encouraged me to read. I felt that God had led me to attend that event.

Over the next several years, I was determined to seek God's will for my life, and to grow in my faith. I felt that God was leading me in a direction of leadership within my own church. I appreciated the friendship of my Lutheran friends, and there was a time that I considered leaving my own church and attending Skudesnes Lutheran Church in Loreburn, where my friends attended. As I prayed about that decision, I felt that God spoke to my heart, telling me that I would be used in my own church. That feeling was very strong, so I started searching for learning experiences.

Because the United Church college, St. Andrews at the University of Saskatchewan, was not accessible, I would not be able to attend any classes there. I enrolled in a night class at St. Thomas More at the U of S: "History of Christianity." I really enjoyed this class, and was excited to learn about the history of the Christian faith. Of course, it was from a Catholic perspective, but it was still about the Christian faith. We still studied Martin Luther, Calvin, and John, and Charles Wesley, among other great people of faith, saints in the Catholic Church. I was interested in some of the ancient fathers of the faith, and also the gospel writers and St. Paul. There was a course offered at Prairie Christian Training Centre called "Laity in Action." It was a three-year course where we met one weekend every other month for three years. Sometimes we were at PCTC, other times we met in different communities around the province. We focused on many different topics: church history, dealing with conflict, interpretation of scripture, Myers-Briggs personality tests and many others. We read different books, wrote papers and even presented sermons. There were times during this learning experience that I really questioned my faith, and also my own church. It was a time of deep searching and struggling to know what I believed and how God was leading me, but I had the strong feeling that God was leading me to be involved in my church.

After I completed this course, I took another from the University of Winnipeg through PCTC to obtain my certificate in theology. Three ladies from my own church met with me monthly and reported to my spiritual advisor from the University of Winnipeg. Following this, I took the two-year lay preachers course at PCTC. It was several years of learning. George and I took turns being away. He was very involved with municipal government as vice president for villages in SUMA as I was taking classes in the church. Along with these learning experiences, I was a member of presbytery and served on the education and students committee in Moose Jaw Presbytery, and then one term on the Conference Stewardship Committee, getting to attend a stewardship meeting in Toronto.

These were busy years as our children were growing up and becoming very involved in their school and sports. As I look back, I wonder sometimes how we managed all the things we did!

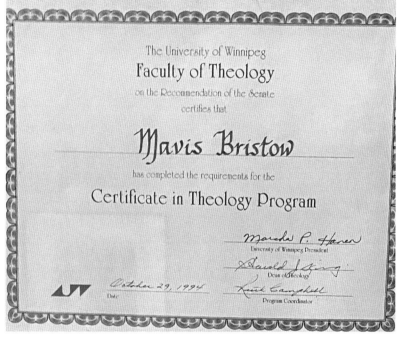

The University of Winnipeg
Faculty of Theology
on the Recommendation of the Senate
certifies that

Mavis Bristow

has completed the requirements for the

Certificate in Theology Program

Marcia P. Haren
University of Winnipeg President

Harold J. King
Dean of Theology

October 29, 1994
Date

Kent Campbell
Program Coordinator

My certificate in the Theology program.

Chapter Thirty-Six

A Special Holiday

In the summer of 1986, Expo 86 came to Vancouver. Donald was done school and working in Saskatoon, helping on the farm and practicing football with the Saskatoon Hilltops, a junior football team in Saskatoon. George and I, along with Alana and Cameron and friends of ours, Ross, Gerri and their daughter, Alison, planned a summer holiday to attend Expo 86. We have many memories of the wonderful trip. Expo 86 was a world's fair held in Vancouver. It was an exposition on transportation and communication, and a wonderful experience. We got a motel close to the fairgrounds. George would have us all up early, and we would be at the gates lined up before they opened. One day, we wanted to get to a certain venue early, and when the gates were opened I hurried in, rolling as fast as I could. It was downhill, and a security man ran after me, telling me not to hurry, that a person in a wheelchair and their entire party were ushered in a special door to private seating. We laughed about our whole party having special privileges because of me. I was also invited to try out a special lift that went up and down stairs. It was very much like the lift at our church in Strongfield, but of course a much better model than our rough one, and much safer.

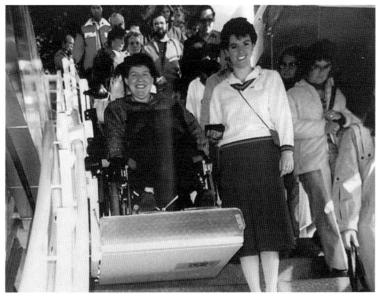

At Expo 86, they were demonstrating new
lifts that go up and down stairs.]

Chapter Thirty-Seven

Our Children

Donald was involved in football as a member of his school team, the Loreburn Aztecs. He played basketball at school and hockey with our local team, going through Novice, Atom, Peewee, Bantam and Midget. He was a good skater and a pretty good hockey player, but in his last year of Midget, after the football season was over, he decided to play basketball instead of hockey. His dad couldn't understand this, because hockey was the number-one sport in the small communities. Donald was tall and slender. I often felt sorry for him, because he was the tallest player on the ice and many on the opposition teams loved to hit the "big guy." Because he was slender, they would knock his feet out from under him and down he would go. His height was to his advantage when he was playing basketball.

Donald excelled in football, and also in track, in the races and especially the throwing events. He won the provincial gold medal in discus in his Grade 12 year. His Loreburn Aztec team won provincials in football that year also. Donald was picked to take part in the first North–South provincial game and played at Taylor Field in Regina. He then went on to play with the Saskatoon Hilltops, a junior football team, during his first year of university. After junior he played with the University of Saskatchewan Huskies. He went to the CIS Vanier Cup in Toronto with the Huskies. In an exciting game against the St. Mary's Huskies in 1990, Donald made a tackle on the quarterback which caused him to fumble the ball in the final minutes of the game. The Huskies recovered and brought the Vanier Cup to Saskatchewan. What an exciting experience for us to watch that game in the SkyDome in Toronto! George and I made many trips throughout the province, and also in Alberta, to watch Donald's games. We stuck it out in all kinds of weather—rain, hail, sleet and snow. We endured each of those conditions while sitting at a football game. I must say, we may not have always enjoyed the weather, but we were always so proud to watch him play football. Even though his football career didn't extend beyond university, there were doors that opened for his career as a financial advisor.

Donald graduated with a Bachelor of Commerce and majored in finance. He has done very well in Saskatoon and area. Donald married a beautiful girl from the nearby town of Kenaston. Susan and Donald are very active in their church. Susan is very thoughtful of others and is always volunteering to help someone out in some way. They love to travel and have had many exciting trips to Hawaii and the United States. Donald enjoys NFL football and loves the opportunity to see a game in Denver! Donald and Susan have three children, a boy and two girls: Joe, Danni and Alli. All of them are active in sports.

Alana was a very conscientious student in school. She did well because she worked hard. She also loved sports, but we always seemed to be going in different directions with the boys playing hockey, so sometimes I feel she was cheated. She did do a little figure skating, and at one time I put her in a summer figure skating camp in Saskatoon with my friend's daughter. She liked it, but we never pursued it. She also tried playing ringette. When she got to high school, she began playing volleyball, a game she excelled in. She also enjoyed high school curling and did very well in that.

From the time Alana was quite young she was very sensitive and tender-hearted. If George and I argued, Alana would become very upset and tell me that she didn't want us to get divorced. When she went to bed at night, she would often dream and then walk in her sleep, so George or I would have to lead her back to her room and into bed. Sometimes I would visit friends who lived across the road, and we might have a beer on a hot afternoon. This would really upset Alana, and she would scold me and tell me not to have more than one!

Alana became a committed Christian as a young woman, but I always said she was a believer from an early age, thinking deeply about things. She has lived out her faith, being very kind and thoughtful of other people and going the extra mile to do things for others.

When Alana left home, she went on to school in Calgary. She stayed with Merla and took fashion merchandizing at Mount Royal in Calgary. She also worked at the Reitmans store in Market Mall. Halfway through the year, she phoned and asked if I would be upset if she switched to athletic therapy. I remember telling her that no amount of education was a waste, and if she wanted to switch it was up to her. She got her athletic therapy certification and hoped to go into physiotherapy, but after an interview at the University of Saskatchewan she was not accepted because she didn't have a degree. She was devastated. I suggested taking a massage course, and maybe later trying again to get into physiotherapy. She began to study massage. Because of me being in the chair she was always interested in physiotherapy. As a massage therapist, she specialized in sports massage and even took courses in infant massage. There were several summers that she volunteered at the triathlon in Penticton BC. She really enjoyed doing sports massage. She worked for many years at the Calgary Winter Club as a sports massage therapist. She volunteered at a lot of sporting events.

Alana got married later in life to Scott Rohatyn. Scott is an environmental agrologist, which is the study of agricultural and environmental science and technology. He complements Alana in many wonderful ways. He is easygoing and very committed to his boys, Nevan and Declan, and to his job. Where Alana was always very punctual like her dad, Scott has helped her to relax. Scott and Alana became busy parents with their two boys.

Cameron, our youngest, is a St. Patrick's Day baby. Because he was born on St. Patrick's Day, he always got a green shirt or something similar for his birthday. When he was very young, we soon found out that he didn't like green, unless it was a John Deere tractor! He definitely had a mind of his own and would not wear a green shirt. In fact, if he didn't want to do something it was very hard to change his mind. I would often try to get him to take out the garbage. I would push him and throw the garbage, but he never did pick it up.

Each of the children took piano lessons. Donald and Alana took them for many years, but I fought with Cameron to practice, sitting beside him trying to make him practice his music. I finally gave up. He did, however, play the drums in the school band after Grade 5, and he enjoyed it. We bought him a set of drums, and he would often sit downstairs, turn on the stereo and play along.

Like both Donald and Alana, Cameron loved sports. He was very particular and had to dress appropriately for the sport he was playing. His favourite was hockey. When we put skates on him as early as two years old, he began running on them and was playing organized hockey before he turned three. They needed all the little ones in the village to have a little Mites team. The refs would carry these little guys out and set them in the proper position for the faceoffs, and parents and grandparents, along with many others in the community, stood around the boards and cheered them on. The rink was a busy place in the winter, with women in the kitchen making burgers and homemade pies on display to attract the eyes of the people around the rink.

George often went to the rink to flood it or do some work, and he would take Cameron with him to skate while he worked. Cameron would spend hours skating and shooting the puck. When he wasn't at the rink, he shot the puck in our kitchen, leaving black marks on the walls and baseboards.

Cameron loved to have friends come to play. He especially loved to have Shane Langager and his brothers come, because they would play shinny outside or go to the rink, but he was shy going to other homes. I was friends with Sylvia, Shane's mom, and I would like to go to her place for coffee. Sylvia was popular, and there were often other women there. If we drove in her yard and Cameron noticed another car in her yard, he'd say, "Please Mom, let's go home." He didn't want to go in, but I would get out and leave him to think about it. Shane would go out to get him, and he was soon playing with the other kids.

When Cameron was a teenager, he was invited to the Victoria Cougars junior hockey camp in Victoria, BC. The camp was in August, when George was getting ready to run the combine, so he couldn't go. Alana and I went out to Victoria with him. We picked up Merla in Calgary to go along with us. The camp was a week long. At the end of the week, we were all shocked when Cameron announced that he was staying. He had made the team. We never believed that this shy boy would stay so far away from home. That was the beginning of his hockey career. He played for the Victoria Cougars, the Melfort Mustangs and the University of Saskatchewan Huskies, and then he went to Europe and played with Norway and Scotland. He met a lovely girl in Saskatoon while playing hockey with the Huskies, and he was married in the summer before going to Scotland, where he played for three years. His wife, Devre, always encouraged him in his hockey and everything else he did. She was great at building up his confidence. He played for Norfolk, Virginia, and Las Vegas in the United States. Cameron now lives in Saskatoon. He and Devre have three children, Warner, Connor and Payton, and Cameron works for Colliers Commercial Real Estate.

Chapter Thirty-Eight

Rocky Roads

George and I raised our family and enjoyed following them in their sports and other activities. We did our best to make our lives the same as other young families growing up in Strongfield. When George was not busy on the farm, we liked to travel to Calgary and visit with my sisters. I wanted Donald, Alana and Cameron to get to know their cousins. They would see them at Mom and Dad's house in Saskatoon, but there were fun times in Calgary also.

Being away from home sometimes brought challenges. My sisters did what they could to help me manage in their homes. When I was young, I was strong. It was nothing to manage in a bathroom on the main level of the house. I easily got down into the bathtub and lifted myself out. Getting in and out of their houses brought with it the challenge of stairs. Merla, Karen and Vicki learned how to pull me up the stairs, and they were good at it. I never feared that they might drop me—I always had confidence in them. There were even times when they would take me down a long flight of stairs into the basement. Karen lived in a split-level house, so when I visited her it was up a flight of about six stairs to the bathroom. I always had complete confidence in Karen, but one time the rubber handle on my chair came off and I went careening down the stairs. The result was only a broken finger, crooked to this day! Eventually Merla and Harold moved to a new home, and Harold put a lift in his garage so that I could get in and they didn't have to pull me up the stairs.

After a fun time in Calgary, we would pack up the kids in the car and head home. We had our favourite stops where bathrooms were accessible. I was always very sensitive to smell. If I smelled manure in the fields, I would check to see if I may have had an accident with my bowels—always my biggest fear. Although I managed quite well, there were occasionally difficult times. We would be driving along, the kids in the backseat, when I would smell something. I first checked the kids when they were little. If it wasn't them, I would accuse George of passing gas. If it wasn't him, I would have realized my biggest fear. I would ask him to pull off on a side road. After being away for a period of time, a change in diet and difficulty getting to the bathrooms were reasons for my bowels to be irregular. We usually carried a pail and rags along with a change of clothes. This one time, we stopped by a slough on the side of the road and let the kids out to run up and down a prairie trail road where there wasn't expected to be a lot of traffic. George was so kind to fill the pail of water from the slough. I got on the floor of the back seat of the car and, with the rags and water in the pail, proceeded to clean myself up while George stood out beside the car and watched the kids. I always did my best to tackle these difficult times on my own, not wanting George to have to help me. As I got older and needed help, he was always so patient with me. I couldn't ask for anyone to love and care for me more.

There were times when George wasn't with me and I had to manage on my own. There were embarrassing times when I was in Saskatoon by myself, or only with my children, but I was fortunate to have Mom's place to go to. After I didn't have Mom living in her home anymore, as she had moved into a condo, I was always fortunate that I often had someone to turn to, but there were times when I would have to head home. After an accident with my bowels, I could invariably count on a bladder infection. The urine becomes cloudy and there is an odour. I usually try to drink lots and take cranberry pills, but in about two days I'm trembling, hot and cold, with a headache. It is then time to see the doctor to get antibiotics.

In my later years, after we retired in Saskatoon, I have had struggles with constipation, and the bowels have become lazy. Using a suppository often brings on an accident, but trying to release them on my own is a huge struggle also. Arthritic hands don't make it easy, but I still manage. Many times, I sit in the bathroom for long periods. Sometimes the tears run down my face, and I sing Dick Damron's song "Jesus, It's Me Again," in which he writes about being down on his knees, asking Jesus to please reach out His hand. Or the spiritual "Nobody Knows the Trouble I've Seen"— nobody knows but Jesus. I turn to Jesus in these difficult times. Often, I might have long periods of success, of which I am very thankful. Establishing a routine is so important. When something happens and upsets the routine, long periods of struggles with the bowels often occur.

Not too many years ago, my granddaughter, Danielle, told me that I should go to see the movie *The Upside*. It is the story of a quadriplegic and his caregiver. At first, I didn't know if I wanted to go, but I asked a friend to go with me and I really enjoyed it. I could identify with much of his life, even though I'm a paraplegic and do have the use of my hands. One thing that really struck me was when the main character talked about his body being on fire. I knew what he was talking about, but I had always described it as pins and needles through my legs and in my seat. Those were days when I seemed to be very agitated. I never knew what caused them, but I always tried to figure out what my body was trying to tell me. What was wrong? Fortunately, I don't have too many spasms, but when I do I try to determine what is causing my legs to jump. Are my bowels or bladder full? Is my shoe too tight, or what might the problem be? Living as a paraplegic, I have always paid particular attention to my body when something seems different.

Other difficult times that I have experienced are not physically but emotionally hard. I don't think they bothered me as much when I was younger, but as I grew older they began to. When I attended the hockey games of my grandchildren, or the occasional concert, I would have to sit alone. There is usually a designated spot for wheelchairs. Others in my family would sit together and visit, but I was all by myself, or with other disabled people whom I didn't know. I yearned to be with others in my family, or with friends. George would sit with the others, visiting. He loves to be with company, and is always meeting new people. I would be by myself. Of course, this is a little thing and something I forget in a short time!

I have always loved a shopping trip. Many times, I have shopped with my sisters in Calgary, and years ago Mom and I shopped in Saskatoon. My friend Gerri from Loreburn and I often took trips to Saskatoon to shop. On one such trip, we had gone over to Second Avenue to look around some of the ladies' shops and were returning to the plaza. The walk light came on and Gerri was hurrying, pushing me across the street. We hit a hard ridge of snow pushed up against the ramped area of the sidewalk, and I flew out of my chair. Before we could blink an eye, two men came out of the door of the Royal Bank and hoisted me back into the chair. Gerri and I thanked them, and have shared many giggles about that experience! Thankfully, there were no broken bones.

I always loved to go places with other women: concerts, musicals, shopping or movies. It was often up to me to organize these outings. I don't know if it was the necessity of having to have the wheelchair along or the concern of me getting into someone else's vehicle, but there were times I felt left out when I heard of a group of women going places. I needed to be the one who offered to drive. Now, as I am older, I take my van with the lift, because it is difficult to get into other vehicles.

Chapter Thirty-Nine

Good Times, Bumps,
New Chair and Cushion

2003 was a year of struggles, as our whole community mourned the loss of a very special person. Sylvia had been such a wonderful friend to me and many others in our community. Everyone was Sylvia's friend. She was one of my greatest supports at the time of my accident, bouncing into the hospital room with balloons on my birthday and appearing unannounced at my door many times, with food, a little book or some goofy thing that we laughed about, like a rubber chicken. Many times, she pulled me up the steps and into her house for coffee, but sat down halfway up the steps, laughing and wetting her pants! She and I and some other friends enjoyed thinking of pranks to pull on each other to acknowledge birthdays. There were many crazy things we did to each other. For Sylvia's fiftieth birthday we got fifty goldfish to put in her bathtub, but her husband found out about our plan and put a stop to it. We ended up getting an aquarium containing fifty goldfish and putting it on her island counter. She enjoyed them until she returned them to our teacher friend in town. That was just one prank out of many. When friends get together to this day, Sylvia's name always comes up.

In March of that year, we also mourned the death of our sister Marge. Marge had been fighting cancer for a while. Merla, Karen and Vicki visited her regularly, and it was very hard for them. She was always such a fun part of family gatherings. I had brought her a special Precious Moments ornament when we returned home from a trip to Virginia.

When I was in Calgary for Marge's funeral, I had been feeling miserable myself, but didn't really know what it was. My stomach had been upset and I was having spells of dizziness. After I got home, I had several doctor appointments but it didn't seem to clear up. I was also doctoring for a little red sore on my hip, which the doctors did not think was a pressure sore. The homecare nurse, Judy, who was a good friend, kept coming and checking it. It would get better, but then come back. I went to my doctor in Saskatoon, and also to a doctor in Outlook. On the day of my sixtieth birthday in May I was feeling really miserable. Friends dropped in for coffee and brought me cake. There were five cakes on my kitchen counter, but I couldn't even look at them. I was so dizzy, and I could hardly see straight. Judy, who had come for my birthday, came back the next day to check my sore and see how I was feeling. She pressed on the sore, and white pus shot across the room. She said, "Mavis, we're going to the doctor!" We went to Outlook, and the doctor put me in the hospital. I was in for a couple of days before they decided to send me to a plastic surgeon in Saskatoon. The surgeon lanced the sore and cleaned out the infection. The doctors determined that there were bone chips in my hip that had been there for a long time, and they had calcified and become infected.

During these two months, while I was feeling miserable, our children and I decided that we were going to surprise George on his sixtieth birthday, which was coming up eight days after mine. George was well known in the area after being mayor of the village for many years, and he was well known in the province from being on the SUMA board and executive. Our children got the word out to many people. They planned a huge celebration to surprise their dad, and they had fun making the plans. I was still in the hospital when the day arrived. We asked if I could get a pass to come out for the event. Alana came, and she, George and I went out for supper in Outlook. Then we drove to Strongfield, because she told her dad that there were some friends dropping in for cake and coffee. When we drove into town, there were many cars at the hall. George always knew what was going on in the village, and he couldn't believe there was something on at the hall that he didn't know about. He asked Alana to stop at the hall so he could check it out. People poured out of the hall, singing Happy Birthday. There were almost one hundred people—not just from our area, but the whole province. There were SUMA board members, relatives from Saskatoon and Calgary and even his cousin from Langley B.C. The kids had managed to put something over on their dad. He talks about it to this day. He loved every minute of it, and couldn't believe that they had surprised him!

I had to return to the hospital for a week or so, because the sore on my hip needed dressing and care every day. After I got out of the hospital, Alana felt that I wasn't sitting as straight as usual. She felt that the left hip was bigger. Ever since I was first in the hospital, the cushion I used in my chair was made of foam. I would buy a piece of upholstery foam and then buy material and make my own cushion. The chair I had at that time was a wheelchair I had purchased. It had touch fastener on the seat (if you don't know what a touch fastener is, you'll have to look it up, as the term I was using is copyrighted), so I would put some more on the cushion cover so it wouldn't slip around when I transferred to it. As the year went on, every time I saw Alana she would try to get me to sit straighter, because she was convinced I was leaning to the right side.

When I was in the Outlook hospital, one of the nurses mentioned something about a Ride® cushion. She said it was supposed to be good at preventing pressure sores. I went online to learn about the Ride® cushion and saw that there was a place in Calgary that sold them. Alana was working in Calgary, so she went to Motion Specialties in South Calgary to ask about the Ride® cushion at the beginning of March 2005. At the end of March, George and I drove to Calgary so that I could see and try one of these special cushions. They just had the standard cushion in stock, but I was told that it would be best if I was fitted for a custom version. I liked the feel of the one I tried and that it was firm, so easy to transfer to.

This began a long process of appointments and convincing doctors and therapists that it would be right for me. The Ride® cushion was not familiar to the medical staff at rehab in Saskatoon. I first had to get a referral from my family doctor. Then—wait! I saw the rehab doctor at the beginning of April, and she agreed that I needed a new cushion. She arranged appointments with an occupational therapist to decide on a cushion and be measured for the right one. I got an appointment with a therapist named Jackie on May 16 at City Hospital in Saskatoon, and I met with her for about two hours. She asked me a lot of questions about my years in the chair and how I managed to do things. She had me try some cushions. She also felt that I needed a lighter chair, but the Saskatchewan government only supplied one make of wheelchair, and they weren't as light as the one the occupational therapist recommended. I told her about the Ride® cushions, and that I had tried one in Calgary and liked the feel and the firmness. I also liked the idea that it was custom made to fit me. Interestingly, she had been to a seminar in California and had heard about these new cushions. I didn't feel that the doctor was totally convinced, but Jackie made some inquiries and found out that there was a seating professional in Regina named Pat who was certified to fit the Ride® cushion, and knew about them. She agreed to contact him and see if it was possible to bring one into Saskatoon. Bob Norrish, my friend in Strongfield, was also interested, because he had trouble with pressure sores. Jackie looked into the Ride® cushion, and because it was not approved by the Saskatchewan government I would have to pay for it.

On June 26, I had an appointment with Jackie at City Hospital, and she had a Ride® r1 cushion for me to try. She took pictures of me on my old cushion and on the Ride®, showing the difference in the way I sat. Jackie wrote many letters to find out what financial assistance was available, but because my accident was before no-fault insurance and I had been paid out a sum of $1000 by Saskatchewan Government Insurance at the time of the accident, there was no funding available. She arranged for me to be sized and have impressions taken to order the Ride® cushion.

On July 20 I had an appointment at rehab in Saskatoon about the Ride® cushion. The rehab doctor was there, as well as my occupational therapist, Pat, the seating professional from Regina, and Steve from Ride® cushions, based out of Denver. I was there for over four hours. First, I tried the standard Ride® cushion, and then they took impressions and fitted me for my own custom version. From what I could tell, it was very comfortable. The first Ride® cushions were made up of many tiny foam beads glued together. When they took the impressions, they put me up in a lift then let me down on soft foam in my chair, which gave them the impression of my pelvis, to see where my ischial tuberosity bones were in the foam. Ride cushions work by selectively loading low risk areas of the anatomy while off-loading high-risk bony prominences. They can also help manage heat and moisture. George and I had decided that we would purchase the Ride® cushion. It was a big purchase, as it was going to cost us $1700, but because I was instrumental in bringing the cushion into Saskatchewan, they gave it to me for $1350.

At the end of August, my new Ride® cushion was ready for me to try at rehab at City Hospital. I was so disappointed! It was way too high in the front and my feet didn't touch the pedals of my chair. I was there all afternoon while Pat, the seating specialist, tried to figure out what to do. Bob Norrish also came to City Hospital that afternoon to be sized for a cushion. My cushion had to be sent back to Denver.

My occupational therapist was also trying to get me a new wheelchair, and we thought the TiLite would be better for my shoulders, as I was beginning to have more and more trouble with them. This chair was not approved by the Saskatchewan government, but Donald was instrumental in pushing for the lightweight chair. Through the generosity of some of my family members, a new lightweight chair was ordered. They felt it was best if the new cushion was fitted into the new chair, and finally, on November 9, I had my new chair and new Ride® cushion. What a huge difference it made to the way I sat.

The first cushion of foam beads was quite heavy, but I got used to putting it in my chair and getting in and out of the van. My newer one is much lighter, and the process of measuring and making the impression is all done by computer. It is quite amazing. The cushion is also very light compared to the first one, and it is made of foam.

Excerpt from my journal
Sept. 2002

You Defy All the Rules

It was a beautiful morning, just the kind that I love. The sun was warm and there was no wind. I wore light-coloured pants and a short-sleeved T-shirt, proof that it was a beautiful day because I am always cold and usually wear a sweater. I felt good. I lifted my chair into the van as I headed off to Saskatoon for my appointment.

I had dragged my feet a little before leaving. I wished that someone could go along with me. George was busy at the farm. He loved to be busy. I thought of asking a friend to go along with me but then I thought that it wouldn't be fair to ask them to wait around for me all day, and deep down I didn't want rejection. Even though I realized that my friends had their own things that they needed to do, there was always a part of me that didn't like to hear for any reason that they couldn't go. I also wished that I had a sister in the city who could meet me, or even my daughter to meet me for lunch like I had so often met my mom over the years. But as I turned onto the highway heading for Saskatoon I felt free and independent and I loved the drive into the city.

There were many things for me to do today. I was hoping to see my grandchildren, and my mother would be waiting for me to come. Mom is nearly 98 years old and lives in a care home. She doesn't have complete care, and continues to be very independent, but she certainly needs help with some things. Her mind is very sharp. She keeps up to date with the activities of each of her family. Her four daughters phone her every evening and her son phones every week or so, depending whether his work takes him away from home or not.

I have two sons in the city. Donald has three children and Cameron has two with another one expected in October. Their families are busy. Donald's son, Joseph, and daughters, Danni and Alli, are ages eleven, ten and eight. They are always busy with friends and activities. Joseph loves sports, like all my family. Donald's wife, Susan, has many friends and is always busy at her church or with her friends and with the children's activities.

Cameron's wife, Devre, owns her own business. She has a Gymboree franchise, which she learned about in Scotland and Virginia and Las Vegas when Cameron played hockey in many different cities. Cameron and Devre's boys are four and two. They both have lots of energy and are busy which means Cam and Dev are busy also.

I got out of the van at City Hospital and got into my chair. I rolled into the hospital and took the elevator up to the seventh floor where I was meeting my occupational therapist. She greeted me with a smile and I followed her back to a room where she wanted to talk to me about a cushion that I was interested in. She had written a letter to send to a government agency to see about funding for a new wheelchair and cushion. She wanted me to read over the letter and see if she had the facts straight. She talked about some of the aids that I had at home to help me. I told her that I used to have a bath every day and lift myself in and out of the tub, but now with a roll-in shower I showered some days and bathed some days and that I had a lift for the tub. She asked if I sat on anything special when I had a bath and I replied, "No, I never had." She said, "You defy all the rules."

I have been in a wheelchair for thirty-eight years. In March I began looking into getting a new cushion and chair. After some surgery on my hip three years ago when some bone splinters calcified and then abscessed, I have one hip that is bigger than the other. This has caused my spine to curve. I had heard about a special cushion that helped a paraplegic to sit straighter. I looked into it on the internet. I went to Calgary where my daughter, Alana, had checked into a company that sold the cushion and she found out about a distributor so I went and tried one out. I was very interested. It was comfortable and I sat up much straighter. I proceeded to talk to my doctor who referred me to a rehabilitation doctor. I was told that I needed an assessment done. In my thirty-eight years in the chair, I had never had an assessment, except maybe when I was first hurt. The last two chairs I had were "Quickies," lightweight chairs I purchased myself, and I had bought upholstery foam and material to make covers and cushions. I didn't really know what an assessment entailed, but I had always managed well. I had never had pressure sores and I had never allowed my disability to really handicap me in any way. I was always very proud of my independence.

As I drove to Luther Riverside Terrace, the senior's residence where my mom lived, there was a smile on my face. The words of the therapist, "you defy all the rules," tickled me. There had always been that little defiant attitude deep inside me that liked to get a rise out of someone or surprise someone. Both the occupational therapist and the physical therapist that I had been going to since having this assessment done had made me feel good about myself. They both expressed amazement at all the things I do as a paraplegic and have always done. I have never suffered from pressure sores, which I attribute to being very active, daily baths, and elastic stockings that I have always worn. There was a time that I did have trouble with bladder infections, but I haven't had one for several years. I am in very good physical condition. Deep down I know in my heart that God has truly blessed me, and I praised God as I drove to Mom's, with a song in my heart.

Chapter Forty

Advocate for Accessibility

W hen I first started to go places in my chair, I never wanted to draw attention to myself. If I couldn't get to a certain place, I didn't go. But George would always insist on helping me get to different places in town. As I mentioned before, his mother would ask people to move so I might see a ball game at the sports ground. She would always make sure I was able to pull my vehicle right up behind the Strongfield Angels' players' bench. I always felt that if people saw me and wanted to move, they would.

When I started to go into Saskatoon, I would park beside an alley so I could get up on the sidewalk, or, if I was in a mall parking lot, I would park on the outside where no one could park beside me. I also thought that as people saw me in public, they would eventually see that changes needed to be made.

Bob Norrish's accident occurred in a truck-train accident in a terrible snowstorm on Valentine's Day, six years after I was hurt. After Bob was confined to a wheelchair, all of a sudden the village realized that there needed to be changes made. Neighbouring towns and villages also became aware of the need to make their public buildings accessible. Hawarden, Loreburn and Elbow, the villages along Highway 19, all started to make their halls, rinks, churches, banks and other buildings accessible. It really helped to make us feel welcome, independent and a valued part of the communities.

As our children got older and involved in sports—curling, hockey and ball—and also attended music events and festivals in some of the bigger centres, I started to write letters to point out where things were not accessible. I always got lovely replies and thank yous from the town councils, government ministers, churches and companies for making them aware of things that weren't accessible. Sometimes change was slow, or made without knowledge of standards and codes, but over the years I have seen good changes and so much improvement. There is a long way to go yet, but governments and many organizations continue to lobby for changes.

In the early years of my paralysis, I wrote a letter to the manager of the Eaton's store in Saskatoon, pointing out that they didn't have a wheelchair washroom. I think they were one of the first big department stores in the city to put in a lovely wheelchair washroom. I got a wonderful letter back from them. I always planned to go to Eaton's on my trips downtown, because I knew there was a wonderful washroom that I could manage and look after my children when they were small.

I wrote to doctors' offices about their buildings and washrooms not being accessible, and the provincial government about the tourist information centre at the Gardiner Dam. They eventually put a hard asphalt path in the sand down to the beach, years after I was finished taking my children to swimming lessons and struggling through the sand in my chair. Now they even have special beach chairs with big wide wheels for one to use when at the beach. How things have changed.

Another avenue I used to make people aware of places that were not accessible was the local Outlook newspaper. I was the correspondent for the Strongfield news in "The Outlook" for many years. I would point out places locally, or in communities I had visited. At our local coffee row, the women used to meet Wednesday mornings. At that time, I would hear stories from others that I could report.

There are so many opportunities now for people with spinal cord injuries. There are many sports: sledge hockey, skiing, water skiing, curling, biking, and opportunities in Special Olympics in numerous events. I often wonder if I would have gotten involved in a sport of some kind if these opportunities were available when I was first hurt. I did try skiing at Whitefish many years ago and loved it.

It has now been over fifty-two years since my accident. There have been many changes. Doctors know so much more about helping patients to stay healthy, and occupational and physical therapists can help patients achieve skills and knowledge about so many new aids and ways of managing and living independently. There are also scholarships available to help people receive an education. The advancement of technology is available for people to obtain knowledge, and to be in contact with others to share and get support. There are peer groups and councillors. I have always been a strong supporter of Spinal Cord Injury Saskatchewan, because they help to put newly injured people in touch with peer councillors and groups, peer support for young mothers and other people who have similar interests. They provide scholarships and make people aware of available support.

I heard a speaker recently talking about the value of meeting with a dietitian to learn the importance of a healthy diet when you are living with a spinal cord injury.

In 2012 I was presented the Queen's Diamond Jubilee Medal by our local MP, Lynne Yelich for contributing to my community.

There are advancements in every area, and professional people to guide you with the many decisions you have to make. There are companies that specialize in equipment and aids to help you live an independent and full life so that you are not so hard on your body.

I certainly encourage anyone who has suffered a spinal cord injury to seek expertise in any area to improve their quality of life.

Minister of Tourism and Renewable Resources
Administration Building, Regina
S4S 0B1

AUGUST 10-17, 1975

July 17, 1975

Mrs. Mavis Bristow,
Box 103,
STRONGFIELD, Saskatchewan.
SOH 320

Dear Mrs. Bristow:

Thank you for your letter of July 6 offering a suggestion that improved access be provided to the beach at Diefenbaker Lake. I expect you have particular reference to the beach area adjacent to the pavilion on Gardiner Dam.

Unfortunately our program for the current season has been fully committed. However, I will be bringing this need to the attention of our Project Development group responsible for landscaping and facility improvement at that location.

Quite frequently these requirements are overlooked. We have found in some instances that such additional installations are beneficial not only for the handicapped but are also of real value to the elderly.

I hope we will be in a position to give serious consideration to your suggestion another year. Thank you for bringing this to my personal attention.

Yours sincerely,

John R. Kowalchuk

A letter written back to me from the government after requesting wheelchair accessibility to the Lake Diefenbaker.

TOWN OF DAVIDSON

INCORPORATED 1906

PHONE 567-2040
BOX 340
DAVIDSON, SASK. SOG 1A0

April 4, 1988

Mavis Bristow
Box 103
Strongfield, Sask.
SOH 3Z0

Dear Madam:

The Davidson Town Council would like to thank you for your letter of March 5, 1988, regarding wheelchair accessible washrooms. Partly as a result of your letter, we will be advising next week for tenders to construct 2 wheelchair accessible washrooms in each of the Town Hall and the Curling Rink. Hopefully, this problem will soon be addressed in our skating ring and other town businesses.

We apologize for any inconvenience the lack of facilities may have caused you and we hope the next time you visit our town you will find that some improvements have been made.

Yours truly,

Gary Edom
Administrator
GE:GB

A letter I received from the town of Davidson after I requested wheelchair accessible washrooms in the town hall and curling rink.

UNIVERSITY HOSPITAL
SASKATOON SASKATCHEWAN
POSTAL CODE S7N 0W8   TELEPHONE (306) 343-2712

October 27, 1976.

Mrs. Mavis Bristowe,
STRONGFIELD, Saskatchewan.

Dear Mavis:

Thank you so much for speaking to the teen volunteers (Candy Blues) on Saturday, October 23rd.

Some of their comments on the evaluation forms under the question, "What parts of the program did you find particularly useful?" were:

- "meeting Mavis and talking with her about her experiences".
- "when Mavis came, I learned how to respond to people in a wheelchair".
- "The talk with Mavis was very useful. Mavis helped me to see that patients feel and we must respect that".
- "The fire explanation was good and so was Mavis".
- "the experience that Mavis told us".

Thank you again Mavis. You were a real inspiration to us all.

Sincerely,

M. Waldner

(Mrs.) Melsie Waldner,
Co-ordinator of Volunteers.

MW:fs

A letter following a conversation with Candy Blues, talking to young teenagers about accessibility and life in a chair.

December 3, 1981

Mrs. Mavis Bristow
Box 103
Strongfield, Sask.

Dear Mrs. Bristow:

On behalf of the Council of the Town of Outlook, I wish to thank you for writing, and identifying some areas that could make some of the areas and facilities more accessible to wheelchair traffic within the Town of Outlook.

More specifically, the washrooms at the Civic Centre, and I am happy to advise you that one door in each of the ladies and mens washrooms shall be replaced with larger doors and steel bars placed on the wall for convenience of maneuvouring around.

The sidewalk improvements have been approved and shall be done in the spring.

Thanks again for bringing this to our attention.

Yours truly,

L.W. Zarubiak,
Town Administrator.

OUTLOOK REGIONAL PARK

GARDINER DAM

IRRIGATION

A letter from the town of Outlook after I notified them of the lack of accessible washrooms and ramped sidewalk curbs.

My team and me at the annual wheelchair races.

Chapter Forty-One

Mom

The greatest influence in my life would have to be my mother. In her quiet way, she was the strength and solid rock that led me in the direction of determination, faith and an appreciation of others. She taught us kindness and respect, not in a forceful way, but by quiet example.

My mom, Luella, was the second oldest of seven girls. Her family grew up in Saskatoon. She was born in Moose Jaw, but her father worked on the railroad and moved to Saskatoon when she was very young. She did have one brother, but he died as an infant. Mom attended school in Saskatoon. Her family lived at 422 Ave. I South. Well, I remember staying at my grandmother's house: the wooden staircase and how we loved to play there, the old gramophone and some of the songs on the old records. I still sing them. I remember the icebox in the kitchen, and when the man would come with a big block of ice and we would have to get out of the way while he rushed in, carrying it with a big pair of tongs to stick it in the top of the icebox, while Gramma stood there with the door open. I remember hearing the *clip-clop* of the horses' feet as the milkman delivered to the door. We were always interested in how the milkman would get out of the cart with his bottles of milk and the horse would go on to the next house, stop and wait for him there. Grandma would leave the empty milk bottles sitting outside the door with the money in them. The milkman would exchange the empties for full bottles of milk.

Mom told us about attending King George school, then walking across the old traffic bridge on cold winter mornings with the wind blowing off the river when she attended high school at Nutana Collegiate, before completing her Grade 12 at Bedford Road. She then attended normal school on Avenue A to become a teacher.

Her first school was near Windthorst, which she went to when she was nineteen years old. She stayed there for one year, living with her uncle and aunt on her mother's side while teaching. The following year, she taught in Broad Acres. After a year there, she went to Asquith, which she enjoyed. She was there for six years. She played the organ for church and enjoyed playing tennis and bridge. After four years, she thought it was time for a change and applied to the town of Imperial, Saskatchewan. When they phoned Asquith for a reference, the man they contacted on the board told them she wasn't leaving, so she stayed for two more years. She then ventured north to Sturgeon River for a year. She often told us the story of the place that she boarded in. It was filthy. There were cats on the table, drinking cream from a pitcher that wasn't put away. Dirty dishes were always around. She stayed the year, and then went to Melfort for a year, but didn't really enjoy it there. Then she went to Perdue for four and a half years. Once again, she played the organ for church, and also enjoyed playing in an orchestra with a local musician, Alvin Oaks. They played for dances around the area. She loved the dances as she had at Sturgeon River. That is where she met my dad, Warner, at a dance. He followed her to Perdue and began working in the grain elevator in Rockhaven after the one in Holbein burned to the ground. Mom married Dad at Christmas, and they went to Rockhaven. She did some substitute teaching in a one-room school with Grades 1 to 12.

Mom and Dad soon moved to Preeceville, two years after Merla and I were born. She didn't teach when we were a young family. After Kent was in school, she went back teaching in country schools around Preeceville. She taught in Chechow, Norway, Hryhoriw and one other. In 1961, we moved to Saskatoon. She began teaching at Prince Philip School and stayed there for nine years. She taught the Grade 1 class. I remember her bringing books home from school and working late into the night. She would cut out pictures, make charts and correct many books, along with the other activities she prepared for her students. Because of her love for music, she taught them many little songs. She also played the piano for concerts and worked with Verla Forsyth, the music person who came around to the school. Interestingly, Verla was a student of Mom's in Asquith.

Mom suffered with Meniere's disease in her forties and lost the hearing in her right ear. Meniere's disease is a disorder of the inner ear that causes spontaneous episodes of vertigo—a sensation of a spinning motion—along with fluctuating hearing loss, ringing in the ear (tinnitus), and sometimes a feeling of fullness or pressure in the ear. In many cases, Meniere's disease affects only one ear.

Because of this, Mom would give students a great deal of individual attention, because she could hear better when she was talking one on one. Mom never let on about her hearing difficulty, and we often felt bad when we were all together visiting and realized that she was being left out of our conversations. We would then quickly talk a little louder and look at her so she could read our lips. She never said that she read lips, but we all felt she did to a certain extent.

When we lived in Saskatoon, we always got together on weekends with Mom's two sisters who lived in Saskatoon. The men would usually get together to play crib, while the women gathered around the piano for a singsong. Mom would be on the piano and Aunt Adell sometimes played the violin. Aunt Doree occasionally took a turn on the piano. We had a great time singing many popular songs and hymns. To this day, I recall the words and tunes to so many wonderful old songs. My daughter will say, "Do you know a song for everything, Mom?" My mom taught us many lessons with music or poetry. It was often a line from a song that she would use to teach us things. Even after she retired, she was always a teacher, correcting our grammar or our spelling. A poem that Mom often recited was the following one by Henry Cuyler Bunner. It often came to mind when I thought of being in a wheelchair, and wondered if it did for Mom too!

One, Two, Three!
By Henry Cuyler Bunner

It was an old, old, old, old lady,
And a boy that was half-past three;
And the way that they played together
Was beautiful to see.

She couldn't go running or jumping,
And the boy, no more could he;
For he was a thin little fellow,
With a thin little twisted knee.

They sat in the yellow sunlight,
Out under the maple tree;
And the game that they played I'll tell you,
Just as it was told to me.

It was Hide-and-Go-Seek they were playing,
Though you've never have known it to be—
With an old, old, old, old lady,
And a boy with a twisted knee.

The boy would bend his face down
On his one little sound right knee,
And he'd guess where she was hiding,
In guesses One, Two, Three!

'You are in the china-closet!'
He would cry, and laugh with glee—
It wasn't the china closet,
But he still had Two and Three.

"You are up in papa's big bedroom,
In the chest with the queer old key!"
And she said: "You are warm and warmer;
But you're not quite right," said she.

"It can't be the little cupboard
Where mamma's things used to be—
So it must be the clothes-press, Gran'ma!"
And he found her with his Three.

Then she covered her face with her fingers,
That were wrinkled and white and wee,
And she guessed where the boy was hiding,
With a One and a Two and a Three.

And they never had stirred from their places,
Right under the maple tree—
This old, old, old, old lady
And the boy with the lame little knee—
This dear, dear, dear old lady,
And the boy who was half-past three.

Mom and Dad's retirement years together in Saskatoon were happy ones. They enjoyed many good times golfing with Aunt Adell and her husband Uncle Bert at the Wildwood Golf Course, and also out at Pike Lake with Aunt Doree and Uncle Allister. The six of them enjoyed many good times together. Mom, Adell and Doree would also enjoy a game of tennis at Pike Lake, and then we would gather for a potluck supper. They were great family times.

Dad passed away in February 1976. In his later years, he had glaucoma. One of the hardest things he did was to give up driving. Dad loved his Buick. He always had it shined up. When he was having trouble seeing, he decided on his own to give up his licence. Mom would drive. She didn't like it, but she did it after Dad felt he couldn't anymore. He began to suffer with emphysema and would get up in the night struggling to get his breath. He went into the hospital in February. I went up to see him one day, to help him eat his meal. A nurse came along, took a hold of my chair and wheeled me out of the room. I was too timid to stand up to her, and I left. That moment has haunted me, because I have often wondered if he wanted to know why I had suddenly left. In his last days, we would visit him and sit and rub his legs, because they were cold. Mom was with him every day. He passed away early in the morning of February 18. Mom regretted not being with him, but she was told that he asked for a Sister from St. Paul's Hospital, and she was with him when he died.

After Dad died, Mom got pneumonia and was very sick for quite a while. We took turns staying with her until she was well. My sisters from Calgary came as often as they could. I was only an hour out of Saskatoon and made many trips in to be with Mom. Doree and Adell were also very good at checking in on her and taking her places, or just stopping for a visit. Aunt Adell lived just across the park and would pop in often. They did a lot together.

As the years went on, I did more and more with Mom. We loved our shopping trips, browsing around Eaton's or The Bay, then stopping for lunch in the Eaton's cafeteria or the lunch counter at The Bay. When my children were small I took them with me, but when they were in school I would go into the city on my own. I would take Mom for groceries, or head downtown. As the years passed and she had more trouble walking around, she loved to just hang on to my chair. I was her walker. There were so many times that we went to the mall. She would window shop while I did things I needed to do, or she would try on a new dress at D'Allaird's. When we met later, she would take me to see it and get my opinion. She usually had her mind made up whether to buy it or not, but I can still see her standing in front of the mirror, turning from side to side, putting her shoulders back and standing up straight, tilting her head and deciding if it looked all right. She loved these shopping trips with each of my sisters when they visited from Calgary. When I was with her, we would arrange to meet at a certain place, and when I arrived she'd be sitting on a bench waiting for me. I'd take her to her house, then get back home for my children after school, or to get supper ready for George. In the summers, he was in the field. In the winters, he was doing work for the community, at the rink or around town. As mayor, he was also the unpaid maintenance man.

One day we were at the mall, and I went off to do something on my own. When I met up with Mom, she said, "Come with me. I want to show you what I've done." There was a new seniors' home being built along the river, Luther Riverside Terrace, and Mom had put her name down to move in. She always wanted to make her own decisions about things, and she decided it was getting to be too much to look after her home on Isabella Street.

In January that year, George and I went to Scotland to visit Cameron, who was playing hockey with the Aire Scottish Eagles. When we contacted Mom, we found out that her furnace had gone out on a very cold night. She had wrapped herself up in a blanket and sat in her big blue chair in the living room. This had been one of the memories that caused her to think about moving out of her home. She was over ninety at this time.

As our children got older, I spent more and more time doing things with Mom and being there to help get things she needed. George's mother had passed away in 1989. She was a year older than Mom. George was wonderful to my mom, always willing to do little jobs that needed doing when Kent wasn't available.

It wasn't uncommon for me to make a quick trip to Saskatoon if Mom needed to go to the doctor or had an appointment somewhere, and because I often came into Saskatoon, I took her for her groceries and other things.

Merla, Karen, Vicki, Kent and I looked after Mom for many years. We each made a special effort to help her in many ways. When she was still living in her home on Isabella Street in Saskatoon, my sisters from Calgary would come and stay with her for several days. There were always jobs to do around her home: cleaning windows, painting, pulling weeds, trimming the trees or cleaning up the garden in the fall. We would often all gather at her home and enjoy our times together, Mom being the centre of the gatherings. Kent would be around when there were repairs that needed to be done around her house.

After she put her name in Luther Riverside Terrace, she tried to forget about it and we seldom brought it up, but as spring approached and we knew that her suite would soon be ready, we planned a garage sale to sell things from her house. At first, it was hard for her to think about selling many of her treasured items that had memories of her family wrapped around and within them. She had each of our names on the back of certain things that would be ours, and there were some items for the grandchildren. When the day of the garage sale arrived, we were all at the house to help out. Gradually Mom brought out more and more items to sell, and we laughed together about people who came. We were lucky if we got a quarter for things that were priced for a dollar, but we let them go.

The big moving day arrived. We decided that we would take Mom out for lunch and a drive, and then she would be taken to her new suite. We didn't want her to be present in her home as the furniture was being removed. I would drive her around while my sisters and Kent arranged her furniture in her new suite, to make it look like her old home as much as they possibly could. Mom loved her suite in Luther Riverside Terrace. She loved to have us come and visit her, and she loved to treat us to a meal in the dining room downstairs. She was very happy in her new home.

Many times, I would drive to Saskatoon and go straight to Luther Riverside. At first, she loved to come with me and go to the mall like we always did, but as it got harder for her to walk around, I would get a list of things she needed, then get things for her and bring them back. I also made a habit of making her plates of food at home and freezing them, so that she could just warm a meal in her oven. The one thing she loved was macaroni casserole, so I often made it and took containers to her. Even though it was extra work for me to make many transfers in and out of the van to go and see her, I always made a point of dropping in before I left the city. Each of us phoned her almost every night, and she looked forward to talking to each one of us. She would say, "I haven't heard from Vicki or Karen or Merla!" We knew she sat by the phone in the evenings waiting to hear from us.

Merla had a piano that she lent to Mom that was smaller than her upright one. It fit in her den, so Mom enjoyed being able to play the piano, and we enjoyed being able to sing around it when we came for a visit.

As things got harder for her, she made the decision herself that she should move downstairs to where she would get more care. It was once again a hard decision for her to make, but one she made on her own. When we got her settled in her room in the care section downstairs where she would get all her meals and more attention, she looked at us and said, "I fear I have made a big mistake!" But once again she settled into her new surroundings. The part that she hated worst of all was that she had to share a bathroom. I could certainly understand how she felt, and I strongly feel that the architects who designed this home for seniors weren't thinking when they made people share a bathroom. Seniors who often need to get to the bathroom in a hurry and cannot move quickly need to have an accessible washroom they can get to quickly. Mom had always been very modest, and it was very embarrassing for her to have an accident. Wearing adult diapers was uncomfortable and humiliating.

Mom would look at others in the care home that were often much younger than she was, and she would feel bad for them if their hair wasn't combed. If she saw that their sweater was crooked, or their collar wasn't straight, she would encourage us to go and straighten it for them. Oh, how we laugh now about the many things she worried about or had us do for others. She would say, "Go and fix that for that poor old soul," about someone who was probably ten or more years younger than she was.

When Mom was ninety-nine years old, nearing one hundred, she fell in the bathtub. She was taken to the hospital, and I went to be with her. They moved her onto a ward. She was in a lot of pain, so they gave her morphine. It was terrible, because she started having hallucinations. She would see things crawling on the wall. She was reaching out, trying to grab things. We would sit with her and try to settle her down. Rather than take her to the bathroom, they diapered her and padded the bed. She hated it. Gradually, they lessened the morphine so that she was aware of what was going on, but she still continued to hallucinate. One day we met with a staff member who told us that her name was on a list to be moved to level-four care. Because I had things accessible at my home in Strongfield, we asked if we might take her there to look after until she could get into a care home. We were told that if we took her out of the hospital, her name would go to the bottom of the list. Vicki stood up, put her hands on her hips, looked the staff person in the eye, and said, "You mean to say that, because we love her, you're going to punish us?" The woman left the room. We sat in silence, wondering what to do. She came back in a while and said, "No, her name won't go to the bottom of the list." It didn't take us long to pack up her things and take her to Strongfield. Merla, Karen and Vicki each took a turn, a week at a time, coming from Calgary and looking after her. I made the meals. Kent even took his turn. What fun we had, and what a special time with Mom! She never wet herself or had an accident. She would call in the night, and we would get up and help her to the bathroom. We laughed when we would help her shower and she would tell us that we hadn't dried between her toes. She was with me all of July and into August. She would love to sit out on our deck and watch the little wrens bringing food to the baby wrens in the bird house, and the goldfinches coming to the bird feeder. Each of us treasured that summer with Mom. Even George enjoyed having her with us when he would come in from the field.

In the middle of August, we learned there was a place for her in a home in Saskatoon, so we moved her in. Once again, we were so disappointed in the care she was given. Her mind was always sharp, and she would tell us things that were upsetting to her. They didn't help her to the bathroom. Once again, they put Depends on her. They put a commode in her room, and when she used it, it was often not emptied for a day or two. They would put a piece of foam on the floor beside her bed in case she fell out. This was a huge obstacle for me—being in the chair, I couldn't get into her room. To top it off, she was on the fourth floor, with only one elevator in the building. I would often have to wait for long periods because the elevator was being used for patients. It was not only upsetting for her, it was upsetting for me. None of the staff spoke to me. I guess being in a wheelchair made me one of the residents! I would leave totally frustrated.

One day, a home-care executive came to see me in Strongfield. I told them about Mom and how frustrated I was. They told me that because I was the primary caregiver, I could put her name in to go in the home in Davidson or Outlook.

The beautiful Bessborough Hotel, built on the banks of the Saskatchewan River in Saskatoon, officially opened on December 10, 1935. As a young woman, Mom attended the opening of this famous landmark. She told us about attending the opening, so Kent decided that on her one hundredth birthday we would have a celebration at the Bessborough. Mom was never a person to like being in the limelight. I was the main organizer of her ninetieth birthday, but I received a lot of opposition from her and other members of the family, because she didn't want a celebration with the spotlight on her. It turned out to be a wonderful family weekend, culminating with a golf tournament in Elbow and a brunch at our home in Strongfield.

No one, not even Mom, objected to the hundredth-birthday party. She was now a resident in Porteous Lodge in Saskatoon. We girls went and got her ready for the big party. Merla did her hair, and Karen and Vicki dressed her in a special dress with a beautiful shawl around her shoulders. We took her to the Bessborough, where she sat in a special chair to greet her guests. She was radiant, with a beautiful smile and her eyes lit up as so many came to bring her greetings. There were teachers who she taught with at Prince Philip School in Saskatoon;

girls that helped care for her at Luther Riverside; friends from Preeceville; her nieces and nephews, children, grandchildren and great grandchildren; and friends of the family. Her mind was alert, and she recognized everyone. It was a wonderful celebration. Vicki and Karen had put together a scrapbook of her years of teaching: certificates she had received, pictures of her sisters and family, and poems that she had recited so often as we grew up. She received greetings from political leaders and other dignitaries, which we put on display. It was wonderful to honour her after one hundred years of a wonderful life.

Everyone who came to celebrate with her was happy to extend their best wishes. After an afternoon of tea and dainties, we knew that it had been a big day for her, so we took her back to Porteous. We took turns staying with her for most of the evening. Each member of our family enjoyed supper and visiting with cousins, friends and extended family that came from a distance for the celebration. We all enjoyed a special time together, remembering so many special times.

Soon after Mom's hundredth-birthday celebration, we got word that we could move Mom into Outlook Long Term Care. While visiting with the home-care coordinator in my home, I told her how Mom, each of our family members, and I were very disappointed in the way Mom was looked after at Porteous Lodge in Saskatoon. Also, it was very difficult for me, because to access her room I had to use the elevator, which was often in use for patients. Of course, I was in a wheelchair myself.

I applied to have her moved, and soon got word that there was an opening in Outlook. It was a very happy day when we moved her. When we rolled her in a wheelchair into her new room, her eyes lit up. The room was bright. The thing that pleased her most was that she had her own bathroom. What a happy day it was for all of us. Merla, Karen, Vicki and Kent would come to visit her in Outlook, and then come into Strongfield and stay with George and me, spending their afternoon and evenings with Mom and then driving back to Strongfield. For three years that was our practice, one of them coming each month for a weekend. During the week, I would usually visit her two or three times. I would love to make muffins or cookies in the morning, and then after lunch take a thermos of coffee and a fresh muffin or cookies and get up to Outlook at about two-thirty. Sometimes Mom was still having her nap, and other times she would be sitting in her blue chair. As I rounded the corner and rolled into her room, she would look up and her eyes would sparkle. She would say, "I knew you would come." We would have coffee and a muffin, and talk about the family. She would enjoy the coffee and fresh baking, exclaiming, "This is gooooood!"

Mom enjoyed her time in Outlook, as well as the staff there. We were delighted to see her happy and content. Mom's mind was bright. She had trouble hearing, but if people sat close to her and spoke into her left ear, she could hear, and she loved to have a visit. She watched the TV-news channel regularly, reading the captions at the bottom of the screen so she was always up-to-date with what was happening in the world.

Mom always cared what she looked like. When I would come to visit, the first thing I would do was fix her hair, and when I would leave she would always have me pick a dress for her to wear the next day. She always had one in mind. I would get it out and hang it on a hook next to the bathroom door, so the girls would be able to put it on her in the morning.

At the beginning of November 2011, my daughter was scheduled for surgery. I hated to be away for any length of time, but Mom told me that my place was with Alana. I needed to help her out with her two little boys. George and I drove to Sexsmith, Alberta, to be with Alana. While we were there, I got a call from Outlook that Mom wasn't doing well. I always went right away if I ever received a call. This time the nurse at the home said, "I think you should come." We headed out just after supper on a stormy evening. Merla, Karen and Vicki headed out from Calgary. Mom just went to sleep. We four girls stayed with her all of that day. We held her hand, rubbed her back and talked to her so that she would know we were there. She breathed her last on November 10, 2011. It was hard to believe that the person who had such a tremendous influence on each one of us was actually gone. Kent was there early the next morning. We cleaned out her room and shared many memories. A week later, we celebrated her life at Third Avenue United Church in Saskatoon. Our families were all there, and many of our cousins, friends and people who knew Mom came to celebrate her life with us. When we get together as family, we love to talk about her and remember all the special times we shared. We laugh at the things we did to make her feel special in those last years, and we are each so thankful that we spent time with her and cared for her until the very end.

Chapter Forty-Two

Empty Nest and Full Life Following

I t was hard to have Cameron leave home, the last to leave of our three children, and he left to play hockey in Victoria. The joy was that it was his choice, and he was doing something that he loved. Another reason why we were comfortable having him so far away from home, was that he was billeted with a wonderful family in Victoria. They had three young children who idolized Cameron.

Alana was in Calgary. She began working at the Winter Club as a massage therapist. Because she was interested in sports massage, she often volunteered at sporting events. One event that she was committed to every year was the triathlon in Penticton B.C. She found it amazing to work with these athletes, and admired their skills and dedication. She continued to enjoy curling while in Calgary. Most of all, she loved to keep up with her brothers' sporting events, and would attend any game that she had the opportunity to. She was also involved in her church. Alana is a committed Christian. She worked with young people in her church. She also became very involved with Samaritan's

Purse, travelling to Mexico to distribute shoe boxes one time and to Brazil on a dental mission another. These experiences strengthened her faith.

Donald was playing football with the University of Saskatchewan Huskies the year that Cameron went to Victoria. This was the year that the Saskatchewan Huskies won the Vanier Cup in Toronto. The papers across the country were full of articles about the U of S defensemen, the "country thug" who tackled the St. Mary's quarterback and stripped him of the ball. Saskatchewan recovered it and won the 1990 Vanier Cup. We received many clippings from friends and family across the country about the Saskatchewan boy who had made the tackle that caused the St. Mary's quarterback to fumble the ball so that Saskatchewan would win their first cup. George's chest grew several inches!

I treasured each experience of our three children. They were all becoming wonderful adults, and their futures looked bright.

Personally, I was getting more and more involved in my church, not just locally but at presbytery and conference level. As a member of presbytery in Moose Jaw, I became part of the education and students' committee. As part of this commitment, we did some discernment of people seeking ordination. It was very enlightening, and yet a time in which I questioned much of my own faith. I also struggled with many of the politics and issues in my denomination, but I continued to attend my own church, our vibrant UCW group, and enjoyed leading the junior choir. I learned so much from the words of the songs we sang. Those wonderful songs strengthened my faith. As a member of presbytery, I became part of the conference stewardship committee, and my understanding of the church and insight into some of the church politics widened even more. It was really a great committee. We travelled to different places in the province, and also to Toronto one year for a stewardship meeting. I can remember being impressed with one of the speakers on philanthropy. These experiences broadened my education in the church, but I still felt that much was missing in my spiritual knowledge. I would arrange to have visits with my dear friend and mentor, Ruth Taylor, the Anglican priest who was instrumental in my turning my life around, seeking God and growing in my faith.

Ruth encouraged me to belong to an Order of St. Luke group. OSL is an international healing ministry. If I was to attend OSL meetings and conferences, I would have to risk going on my own. At first, it felt like a daunting challenge. George wasn't interested, and I guess I was hesitant to ask others to join me, maybe fearing rejection, so I struck out on my own. I went to OSL conferences and had to find accommodations that were accessible, but I did it on several occasions. I did take two friends with me to an OSL conference in North Battleford, called "Healing the Whole Person." We each talked afterwards of our individual experience of the Holy Spirit. When I first thought of attending, I hoped for physical healing. I went forward for prayer, but physical healing wasn't to be. The inner peace and acceptance of my life in the chair, along with the confidence that God was providing strength every day and using me as a servant in the church, were the gifts that I received.

In our local church, we experienced an extended time without a minister, and I was called on to lead many services. I was also asked to instruct a confirmation class under supervision from a minister in Central Butte. There were three young people in Strongfield who were confirmed. It was enlightening for me to work with these young people. In this time, I was also asked to do funerals. Many people commented on how they liked my leadership in the funerals I conducted, and I considered it an honour to be asked. Some were people I had known very well, and it was hard to do them, but I know that God gave me a special strength at that time. I would read and pray for long periods for the Holy Spirit to give me some insight into a theme or special scripture to use. I was always so amazed how there always seemed to be a piece of scripture that might relate to an individual's life, whether they were church people or not, and I could always find something positive about them. God always seemed to point me in that direction. Over the years, I have been asked to do many, many funerals. I always felt it was an honour to be asked.

During the early '90s, the organist of our local United Church and a good friend, Carole Norrish, Bob Norrish's wife, and I got together and planned dinner theatres. We invited the Lutheran ladies and others to join with us. We started in September to plan the menu and the food. Carole would write the script. She was a very talented person in many ways, and the script was always humorous. The theme was the "Shady Poplars" nursing home. We would incorporate music and Christmas carols into the production. I would pick out the music. Carole would even write some of the songs. We got another local musician to play the piano. Carole was the director of the play, and I was the director of the music. The people in the play would ab-lib some of the parts, and also learn their lines. They had lots of fun meeting once a week, up until it was presented in our local hall at the beginning of December. With help from all willing ladies in the community, we prepared all the food and decorated the hall. We brought in a huge amount of money that was divided between Skudesnes Lutheran Church and our local United Church. We did this for three years, until Carole became very sick with cancer.

Chapter Forty-Three

Where Have I Seen God in My Life?

O ne of my favourite passages of scripture is Isaiah 6:1–8. Isaiah experienced God, and felt God calling him. He knew he was unworthy, and exclaimed, "I am a man of unclean lips." But God reached out and touched him, and when God asked who he would send to proclaim God's word, Isaiah said, "Here I am, send me!" I can identify with this portion of scripture, because when I first started getting involved in ministry, I felt so very unworthy, but like Isaiah I felt God was calling me. It became many years of seeking God, years of reading the Bible, reading other books and seeking God with all my heart. I found that the more I learned, the more I felt how little I really knew. There was such a vast amount of spiritual knowledge that I would love to understand, and it was exciting. I am still learning!

I think one of the most important things for me is that I realized God loves me. I am far from perfect! There are so many reasons to beat myself up. Every day is a learning experience, and every day I need to recommit my life to Jesus and seek to see him in the people I meet, recognizing that they are also equally loved by God, and sometimes I fail! I have many questions that I don't have answers for. I continue to read and search. Sometimes, my devotion times are sporadic, but I know my life is smoother when I regularly spend those quiet moments reading and praying each day. I have always known that my family loves me. My sisters and my brothers and I are very close. We might disagree on some things, but we never confront each other. We're not the "huggy" type, but we enjoy being together, and we support each other and our differences. My twin sister and I share our faith. We can talk for long periods of time about our Christian commitment, different issues or a portion of scripture. She made a commitment several years after I did, when she was having trouble with a teenager. I told her to get down on her knees and pray about it. She did, and her life changed after that.

St. Augustine wrote, "Our hearts are restless until they find their rest in You." I believe that is so true. We search for so many things throughout our life, and when we realize God's love for us, there is that sense that we are loved and that things will be all right! There may be difficulties, but God will be with you all the way.

One thing I noticed not long after my visit with Ruth, is that I was very conscious about my language. I was very aware of swearing, and I didn't like to use profane language or God's name in vain.

For many years, there was a group of women in Strongfield that met every Wednesday morning for a Bible study. We were from different denominations, and there were differences, but this group of women, varying in numbers, regularly met for about twenty years. There were about four regulars who met consistently during that time. We really learned a lot, and prayed often for our families and for people in our community going through difficult times. We saw healing and answered prayers that we gave thanks for and rejoiced in.

As I look back over my life, I can see that God has been with me all along, and I didn't really recognize that it was Him. The coincidences in my life were really God moments!

One small way I feel that God is revealed to me in a strange, coincidental way is in helping me to find lost items. One might think that is silly, but not too long after I began seeking to know God better, our oldest son lost one of his contacts. I was very concerned, and I prayed that I might find it. I was down in the bathroom later that day after he had gone to school, cleaning the bathroom that he always used. There was the contact stuck on the door of the cupboard under the sink! I was so excited. I had prayed about it. I knew God had answered my prayer. I got into the car and drove to the school in Loreburn to take him his contact. As it turned out, he had to get a new one because it was a soft contact and it had dried out. I was still very excited because I had found it, and felt that my prayer had been answered. Some might laugh and say it was coincidence, but not in my mind!

Three times I have lost the diamond out of my diamond ring, and three times I have found it. The first time I had gotten up in the morning and my ring caught on something. I hardly ever take it off, unless I am making bread or buns or pie pastry, because I use my hands to mix the dough. I looked at my ring that morning and the diamond was gone. I was sick about it. I told George. We looked everywhere we could think of: in the bedsheets, around the kitchen, everywhere! I prayed, and then we forgot about it. The next morning, George was sitting on the toilet. The door was open, and the sun was shining in the east window. Something glittered in the sunshine. He went and looked, and there was my diamond in the carpet. Thankfully, I hadn't vacuumed that day. Another time, my brother and his wife were visiting, and we took them to Elbow for a drive to show them around the area. It was raining when we got home. I came inside and noticed that the diamond was gone out of my ring. We went out beside the car to have a look to see if it was in the car, or beside it from when I transferred out. Every little stone glittered in the light because of the rain, so we came inside. A while later, we once again saw something shining in the carpet in almost the same place as before. There was my diamond! We began to wonder if I was knocking my hand on the door frame when I rolled out of the bathroom, and that was why it was in that spot.

Many years later, in Saskatoon, we took our grandchildren to pizza place for supper. We were supposed to meet their parents later at the bumper cars on Idylwyld Avenue. When we arrived, I got out of the car to watch the kids on the bumper cars having fun. We left them with their parents, then stopped at a big department store where I used the washroom, and then drove home to Strongfield. When I was in the bathroom getting ready for bed, I noticed the diamond was once again missing. Again, I was sick. I felt like I had been hit in the stomach with a brick. I told George once again. I wondered if I should phone the pizza place or the department store and ask if someone would look in the bathrooms I had used in both places. George said that if they had been cleaned, it would have been swept up with the dust and thrown away. I sat on the edge of the bed and silently talked to God, saying, "I know this is silly, Lord—why would you help me find my diamond again? But Lord, I really want to find it." In the morning, I asked George if maybe we should look in the van. He went out to the garage with a flashlight and looked beside my seat and between the seat and the console, and there it was. He came in, held it out to me, and asked, "Is this it?" I couldn't believe it. Once again, I was praising God! In Church on Sunday morning, our minister asked if there were any joys or concerns. At first, I thought maybe people would think I was kind of silly, but I mustered up the courage and I shared about finding my diamond. Now, about every six months, I get my diamond checked by the jeweller to make sure that the diamond is not loose.

I have never had a lot of jewelry that I really treasured, but Cameron and Devre brought me a Celtic cross back from Scotland. It is something that I have always loved and worn often. After we moved to Saskatoon, George bought me some little gold earrings for my birthday. They are small and dainty and I have always loved them. There is white gold in the middle, and a hook that goes in pierced ears. There is nothing on the back of them. One day, I wore them to Dr. Kirby's funeral, the doctor who had always been so good to me after my accident. I stayed dressed up that day after we came home, as we were going to visit friends, Ron and Lynda Colton, that night. I did think maybe I should take them out, but I didn't. When we came home that night, I noticed one of my earrings was missing.

Once again, I felt sick. I phoned Lynda and asked her to look around where I was sitting. She phoned back the next day to say she couldn't find it. I prayed but gave up. A few days later, I was doing laundry, putting clothes in the washer. I glanced at the floor and saw something gold. There was my little earring. Finding it made me more conscious about my morning prayer time and devotions. I felt once again that God was drawing me back to a closer relationship! Like the parable of the lost coin in the gospel of Luke 15:8–10, I want to call my friends together and tell them how God has helped me find the things that were lost.

Of course, when I met with Ruth Taylor at the SUMA Convention back in 1983, it was a time when I encountered the Holy Spirit. My priorities in life changed. I began searching to understand God, and to seek to live a life of faithfulness to Him. I turned forty years old that year, and, as I often said, life begins at forty!

I believe there are angels among us! I was on my way to Lucky Lake one Sunday morning, and George was not with me. I was leading worship that morning. I was driving our big burgundy Ford van. It was a windy morning. All of a sudden, the front hood of the van blew up. I had to quickly pull over to the side of the road. I would have had to get in my chair and get out with the lift, but it was almost impossible to reach up and get the hood down without some help. That was when I met a car travelling in the opposite direction. It pulled over to the side of the road, and a man got out and closed the hood for me. I was so thankful. Not only did it save me the trouble of trying to close it, but it would have made me late for the service.

Another time, I drove to Outlook to visit with my mom. When I was driving home, I rounded a curve in the road just outside of Broderick. There was a steep ditch on the top of the curve, and I was meeting another vehicle. The vehicle behind it lost one of its wheels, and it came rolling toward me at a tremendous speed. I couldn't take the steep ditch, and I couldn't swerve into the vehicle I was meeting. The wheel hit me right in the middle of the front of the van, then bounced over my vehicle and rolled into the ditch. The air bag went off, and I pulled over to the side of the road. I had a cell phone with me at that time. I tried to phone George but couldn't reach him. The next car that I met was a lady from Strongfield, who recognized me. She went up the road and pulled into an approach, then came to talk to me. An RCMP car then came by, stopped, rolled down his window, and told us we had picked a poor place to visit on the side of the road. He then pulled away. After I got a hold of George and was able to drive the vehicle home, we contacted the RCMP and reported the incident. A week later they called me into the police station to report what had happened, and I received an apology from the policeman I had met on the road.

When Cameron was playing hockey in Scotland and he and Devre were living there, George and I made a trip over to Scotland to spend some time with them. I was very anxious about how I would manage in Scotland. I prayed a lot, asking God to be with us during that trip. When we first arrived, I got out of the vehicle outside of our hotel. I backed up on the cobblestone walk, which wasn't even. The chair dropped back and I tipped over, my legs going over my head. I was so sore for a few days, having hurt my ribs.

We toured around Scotland and went to Edinburgh Castle. I was amazed to find that on each floor to the castle there was a wheelchair washroom, and they were all exactly the same. They were very easy to manage in. When we got to the top of the castle, we toured St. Margaret's Chapel. It is very small; it doesn't hold more than about twenty people, and it's very old and lovely. In 1942, St. Margaret's Chapel Guild was started. People with the name Margaret belong to the guild and would regularly change the flowers on the altar. Cameron helped me up a couple of steps into the chapel. There was a special feeling that came over me as I sat inside. I felt the presence of God, and that I was loved and God would take care of me during this trip. After Cameron helped me out of the chapel, they all walked on ahead of me. I sat for a moment and pondered my experience. A guide from the tour of the chapel came out, handed me a little book, and said, "I think you will enjoy this, 'St. Margaret, Queen of Scotland, and the Chapel.'" It is the beautiful story of St. Margaret's faith and her love of the people. I will always treasure that little book as a sign of God's love and presence with me on that trip to Scotland.

When I have been asked to lead worship, I often found that I wouldn't have any idea of what to preach. I would read the scriptures over many times, and sometimes wonder what my theme would be, but God always gave me some inspiration. Sometimes it wouldn't come until Friday night, and sometimes I changed things Saturday night or Sunday morning, but God never failed me. I often think about my high school English and university. I never felt I was very good in English, and my marks were poor. Who would have ever thought that I would be writing sermons? God picks the most unlikely servants! I've often said that when God gets your attention, He doesn't let you go. In the last several years, I've been asked to do many funerals. I found it hard at first, but I feel it really is an honour to be asked to officiate someone's funeral. I have always been so warmly affirmed. I have no doubt that the Holy Spirit was leading me, because almost always the Spirit has led me to a special scripture to use to honour the individual, and given me words to say. When people thank me and tell me it was perfect and they appreciate it so much, I say it wasn't me, it was God!

My involvement with the Order of St. Luke was always a time of inspiration. The people I associated with who were part of the group inspired me. The stories they shared, and the conversation and insight built my faith up. I would drive into Saskatoon for those meetings once a month. We always had a study, a book that we discussed, a speaker or a healing service. I would drive home afterwards on top of the world. It was always a real high! There was one time that I knew I had to lead a funeral, and I was wondering what to preach. I commented on this to Larry Mitchell, our Order of St. Luke chaplain, who said, "Always preach Jesus." I have always remembered that. Jesus is the source of love, compassion and comfort.

I thank God for my health. Over the many years that I have been paralyzed, I really haven't had a lot of bladder infections. I have been quite healthy for most of my life. Many paraplegics are troubled with pressure sores, and I am so thankful that I have never had one. I attribute it to my active lifestyle, and to always wearing compression stockings that have helped my circulation. Every morning I take the time to pull on my compression stockings all the way to my hips. Some mornings it is harder than others, but it has been worth the effort. I also believe that getting in the tub and having a bath often has helped. When we fixed up our bathroom in Strongfield in early 2002, we put a lift into a jacuzzi tub and a roll-in shower. I have a bath three or four times a week. Before we got the lift into the tub, I lifted myself in and out almost every day. I believe that too has helped my circulation. Regular exercise has also been a part of my life. At one time, I got down on the floor and rolled around, and did as many push-ups as I could. When my children were little, they did them with me. Now, in later life, I do them on the bed, and with a group in our condo throughout the week. I thank God that I have been blessed with the determination and insight to do things that I believe have contributed to my health.

So often God has nudged me to do something or go to someone, and I have turned the other way. As I previously mentioned, when God gets a hold of you, He doesn't let go. When I have followed the Spirit's leading, that is when I have felt peace within.

I believe that over the years, as I have grown in my faith, I have learned to have a greater love and compassion for people, and I have learned how to listen to others. I believe that everyone has a story. Everyone has something in their lives that has shaped who they are and how they live their life.

Chapter Forty-Four

Joy Watching
Grandchildren Grow Up

I was fifty-two when I got word that we were going to be grandparents. Of course, I was way too young to be called Grandma! But I was thrilled to think of a little one coming into our family. Donald and Susan were expecting a little one sometime in February. When we got word that Susan was in the hospital in labour, we waited and waited. It was such a long time, but we finally got the call from Donald that he was the proud daddy of a little boy. Joseph Donald Bristow was born on February 15, 1995. They didn't name him right away. There were several names they had thought of. When the name Joseph came up and they learned that it was my brother Kent's first name, they decided to go with it, and his second name was Donald, after his dad and Grandpa Bristow. We rushed into Saskatoon to see this new little one. Susan's mother, Connie, was also there. Getting a chance to hold this little fellow was a real thrill. I still remember his bright little eyes looking back and forth, as if he was wondering, *Where am I?* I was mesmerized by him. I just wanted to watch every little movement. He was perfect. As the days, weeks and months went by, it was a thrill to just see him and hold him. When he got a little older and he was able to sit on my lap, I sewed a little harness out of blue jeans that I was able to tie around my waist so I could hold him on my lap. That way I was able to roll up the street and take him for a ride. Like any other grandma, I was thrilled to be able to show off my new grandson.

The times of having him come to visit didn't seem often enough. When I was a mother to my own children, there wasn't time to just watch them and pay particular interest to the little things, but as a grandma it was delightful to pay special attention to being with Joseph, doing things with him and just watching him. He loved Grandma to draw pictures with him when he was a little fellow. We drew animals, people, cartoon characters, cars and trucks, but what he wanted me to draw most were hockey players, even animals that were hockey players. He would have me cut them out, then he would stand them up and we would paste them along the wall. I had little hockey-player figurines for cake decorating that he would line up in the middle of the floor. He would stand with his stick in hand and sing "O Canada." Then he would drop the puck and run around, saying, "Go, go, go!" He had a team and an opposition placed around the kitchen.

Joseph came to stay with Grandpa and Grandma often. Grandpa was busy in the field or attending to town business, so Joseph and Grandma would spend the day together. Sometimes he stayed overnight. He liked to sleep with Grandma, so Grandpa was sent to the other bedroom.

I don't remember a lot of the cute things my children said or did, but it is interesting how grandmas like to share stories about their grandchildren. One time, Joseph was in the bedroom with me and he noticed egg cartons up in our closet. He asked why they were there. I told him that Grandpa collected golf balls and put them in the egg cartons to save them. He asked, "What do you collect, Grandma?" I said, "I don't really know. I really don't collect anything." He was jumping on my bed as he talked to me. He kept jumping as he said, "I know what you collect, Grandma!" I asked, "What?" and he said, "Dust!" There was dust on the headboard of our bed.

Another time when he was spending the night with us and sleeping with Grandma, I was getting undressed and putting my nightgown on. I had my back to him. I had hurt my arm a few days before and had a bandage on it. He saw the scar on my back from the surgery at the time of the accident and asked about it. I told him, and he responded, "You're a wreck, Grandma!"

A very short time after Joseph was born, we were blessed with a granddaughter, Danielle (Danni), from Donald and Susan. She was sixteen months younger than Joseph. She had dark hair and a little round face. She and Joseph were very close. They loved to play together. Grandpa got a little sandbox and put it right outside the kitchen window so they could play together and I could easily watch them. There was only one problem: Danni liked to eat the sand! We were forever cleaning it out of her mouth. There was also sand in her diaper! We often remarked that in Danni's baby pictures she looks a lot like Grandpa in his. Grandpa has always been very proud that his granddaughter looked like him. She is a bubbly, happy young woman now, and we love to have her come for a visit to brighten up our life.

On Joseph's third birthday, Donald and Susan gave us another little granddaughter: Alexandra (Alli). We loved to have those three little ones come and spend time with us. They all loved to ride on Grandma's lap, often two of them at a time. Donald and Susan would dress them up and bring them for Hallowe'en when they were little, and of course they would come for some time at Christmas. There were also times they would stay overnight, or for a couple days. As I look back over the times they stayed with us, I wonder how I ever managed! Three busy little ones! The girls would love it when I would bake with them. They would be up on the counter helping me, pouring the ingredients into my mixer. They loved to crack the eggs into the cookies, then Grandma picked out the shells. We would often make cowboy cookies, their favourite. They also liked to help me decorate cakes. I found a lot more patience with my grandchildren than with my own children. I think most grandmas can understand what I am saying. Alli was a determined little one, and she wanted to do what Danni did. She was right there, helping out. She liked to play with the ornaments that Grandma had on the lower shelves in her kitchen. When her mom or dad told her not to, she would look at them sternly and remind them that her Grandma had told her she could! When they stayed overnight, they often all wanted to sleep together. They got along so well. They would giggle away until Grandma finally had to get after them to get them to settle down and go to sleep. Often, I would sit outside the bedroom door until all was quiet.

One time, I was outside playing ball with Joe, Danni and Alli. I was the pitcher and Joe was batting at the time. He connected with the ball and it hit me in the leg. Joe felt really bad, but I said to him, "Grandma doesn't feel it, Joseph." That made him feel better. Then each of them kept feeling my legs and asking, "Can you feel that, Grandma? Can you feel that?" It really intrigued them. I did have quite a bruise on my leg for a long, long time.

Another time, when I had the three of them with me, we all went downstairs in my hydraulic lift. The lift had a lever that I pulled when I got to the bottom that let down a small ramp that I backed off of. In their enthusiasm, the kids let the ramp down without realizing that we weren't at the bottom. I backed off and dropped. My legs went up over my head, and I fell out of the chair. Joe, Danni and Alli were really scared! They got down on the floor beside me. I wasn't hurt too badly. Danni and Alli sat on the floor with Grandma, and Joseph went to find Grandpa, who we knew was down the street cutting grass for the village on the village lawn mower.

Someone told me once that if I lived my life thinking I would never fall out of my chair, I wouldn't have much of a life. I have fallen out of my chair many, many times. These things happen, but you have to plan to get back in and go again.

Cameron and Devre decided they would not stay in Scotland another year. There were changes happening to the Scottish Eagles organization. Cameron had also received encouragement to look into playing hockey in the United States in the American Hockey League. He and Devre were expecting their first child. Devre returned home from Scotland near the end of March, and Cameron would return shortly after. It was just in time to be with Devre to welcome their first child. Cameron called us to come and be at the hospital. Devre had been in labour for a long time, and my heart ached when I saw her. Thankfully, her mother, a nurse, encouraged them to think about a Caesarean section. George and I and Devre's mom and dad were waiting anxiously in the waiting room, when Cameron came and stood in the doorway, garbed in a blue hospital gown and cap. He had a big smile on his face. He told Devre's mom and me to come with him. I said, "Take Devre's parents; Dad and I will come after." He could only take two at a time. He said, "No, I'm taking the grandmothers." We went in beside Devre's bed and she held up this little fellow, covered in a white paste. She handed him to me and said, "This is Warner." The tears ran down my face. They chose to use my Dad's name, Warner Cameron Bristow. I never dreamt they would use that name. I was so thrilled.

We were delighted to have the chance during the summer to get to see Warner quite often. Cameron and Devre would come down to Strongfield. Cameron would often help George out at the farm, and I would get the chance to hold Warner when he and Devre would visit. Later that year, Cameron went to Norfolk Virginia to play hockey in the AHL with the Norfolk Admirals. George and I decided that we would make a trip that fall down the East Coast to Virginia to see some of his hockey. It was a wonderful trip. We drove to Ontario. George had cousins in Collingwood and Sarnia. I had an aunt and uncle and a cousin in Thunder Bay. We visited with these relatives, and also cousins of George's from Collingwood, who joined us in Sarnia. After the visit with these relatives, we drove to Virginia Beach where

Cameron and Devre had a condo. The view out their living room window was spectacular. You could see the dolphins swim by in the Atlantic Ocean. We enjoyed getting to know Warner, who was a cute little blond-haired baby, eight months old. He crawled around and loved to sit in front of the TV and wave his hands up and down while watching the "Baby Mozart" videos. We saw several of Cameron's hockey games. One night, we went to a seafood buffet and enjoyed some of the best seafood I've ever tasted.

We left Virginia and travelled west. We stayed one night in Bristol, Tennessee. This is where Tennessee Ernie Ford came from. We went to a local mall in the morning and had breakfast in the food court. We laughed and remarked to each other about all the seniors who were walking in the mall in the morning. We looked in tourists' information to see if there was an exhibit of Tennessee Ernie Ford. We went to the house of his family, but there was really nothing about him, just the address where he had lived. Leaving Bristol, we drove to Nashville. Everything was decorated for Christmas. We toured the Opryland Hotel and got lost in the many corridors. We marvelled at the gigantic Christmas trees covered with lights and decorations inside the hotel. We went to see the place where the Grand Ole Opry was held, and toured the Nashville Predators hockey arena. From Nashville, we went to Memphis to see Elvis Presley's mansion.

We left Memphis and drove to Carthage Missouri, where the Precious Moments figurines are made. We marvelled at the wonderful ornaments and the beautiful little Sistine Chapel. Samuel J. Butcher, the creator of Precious Moments, designed and painted over 5,000 square feet of murals inside, all featuring

Precious Moments characters. I purchased several little figurines for my sisters and some friends. I was so in awe of that little place that I hated to leave, but we left and drove on to Branson, Missouri, where we enjoyed the Christmas decorations and music of many entertainers, especially Andy Williams.

It had been a long, wonderful trip, and now we were anxious to get home, so we drove long hours until we were back in Strongfield.

The next year, Cameron played hockey with the Las Vegas Wranglers. We spent three weeks in Las Vegas and watched many of Cameron's games in the rink connected to the Orleans Hotel and Casino. Warner was over one year old now. We took a little pair of skates with us to Las Vegas. Warner played with a little hockey stick all during his dad's hockey games, and was quite a hit with many spectators. He danced when they played the song "I Want to Drive the Zamboni" over the intercom. We gave him the skates we brought for Cameron to put on him after one of his games. The tears rolled down Warner's face when he couldn't skate fast like his dad!

Warner came to Strongfield to stay with Grandma and Grandpa many times. In fact, Grandpa loved to bring the grandchildren down to Strongfield for a visit. The thing is, Grandpa would bring them down and then he would disappear out to the farm, or into town someplace. One time, I was taking Warner over to a little park in town. Warner loved to run. When we got to the schoolyard, away he ran, his blond hair blowing in the breeze! He ran onto the field, where I couldn't go after him. I just had to wait until he came back. I called him, but it was quite a while before he returned to me. He finally did, a big smile on his face, and we went and enjoyed a time on the swings and slide in the park.

Two years after Warner was born, Cameron and Devre welcomed another little fellow into their family. Connor Mason was born at the end of April. Cameron had decided that they would settle in Saskatoon and he would get a job. He still played lots of hockey with clubs around the province. He played in Eston for a few years, and also in Loreburn with our local club, the Loreburn 19ers. Connor was a very content baby. Our family was growing. Danni and Alli loved these little ones and were anxious to look after and fuss over them. Auntie Sue also loved babies and little ones. No one could bring a smile to a little one's face more quickly than Auntie Sue. They got all kinds of attention when they went to Auntie Sue and Uncle Donald's. Uncle Donald liked to tease. He would get a reaction out of Warner, but no one got much of a reaction out of Connor. He was happy when he could ride on my lap or examine my chair. If I got out of my chair, Connor was quick to crawl into it. Connor was curious, very interested in how things worked. He would take things apart and we would have to look for parts when we wanted to put them back together. Connor was always very concerned about me not having feeling in my legs. He liked to poke me, asking me if I could feel it. He was very easy to look after, content to entertain himself with something.

Potty training was something Connor didn't have any interest in. Devre had to threaten him that he would not be able to go to kindergarten if he wore diapers. That finally convinced Connor that he should go potty. He was then quickly trained. Connor has always been his own person. Cameron and Devre put him in soccer, and he would lie on the field and look at the clouds. They put him in hockey, and he was more interested in the fans. He tried speed skating, and was really good at it, but competition wasn't in Connor's makeup. He tried basketball, but rarely touched the ball. As a little guy, he always had a unique idea for a Hallowe'en costume. He would dress up and act out his character. Connor was a technical person. He could figure out iPhones and all kinds of gadgets. As he grew older, he would save his money to buy the latest new device.

Cameron and Devre's family was complete two and a half years after Connor, when Payton was born. Everyone fussed over another little girl. As she grows older, Payton is keen on everything. She is in synchronized swimming and is very good. We have always marvelled at her dedication. She has early-morning practices, and spends many hours after school and in the evenings at the pool. Her mom has been very involved also, helping out in many ways. Her team has placed first in many shows. She is dedicated and works very hard, even making the national team. She loves almost every sport. She plays softball and is very good at it. I have been pleased that Payton has been interested in playing the sport that I always loved. We have a ball player in the family! She is quick to sign up for everything, and volunteers to help out in many areas. She also loves to bake and has brought Grandma and Grandpa samples to try. She will bake with Grandma when she has time to work it into her busy schedule. We look forward to watching Payton in many high school sports, for we feel she will sign up for as many as possible. She is tall and has the long Bristow legs.

George and I love to see each of these grandchildren whenever we can. When our family gets together, there is lots of excitement and noise. The older ones are excellent with the younger ones, and always happy to have times together. Payton is the apple of her daddy's eye. She knows how to wrap him around her finger. Payton wasn't very old when she became interested in synchronized swimming, which has kept her mom very busy, as Devre is an outgoing person, always ready to volunteer and help out.

Alana married later in life. For many years, I prayed faithfully that Alana would meet someone special. Alana had a deep faith that seemed to always be with her. I even felt she had a deep faith as a little girl. Alana also prayed for the right man to come into her life. Even my Bible study group that met every Wednesday for many years prayed for Alana's future husband. I can look back in my journals and read over and over again prayers for Alana's future husband. Scott and Alana were married in May of 2007, and in May of 2008 their first little boy was born.

We expected him on George's birthday, May 10. Alana went into the hospital that day, and the next day I set out for Grande Prairie, an eleven- or twelve-hour drive. George was busy seeding in May, so I set out on my own. The only problem I encountered was not finding a service station that would pump my gas for me. Just out of Edmonton, there was a little service station as I turned north to Grande Prairie. I saw two or three men standing around outside, so I pulled up and asked if one of them would fill my tank with gas, explaining that I was a paraplegic. Being so incredibly independent, it is hard for me to work up the courage to ask for help, but they were very willing and I felt really good afterwards. I was on my way again. Alana had wanted to have her baby naturally, but that wasn't possible for her. The doctor had to do a Caesarean section. Their firstborn son, Nevan William Rohatyn, was brought into the world. He was a big boy. I think he looks a lot like his mom. Alana and Scott are wonderful parents. They both took turns looking after their baby. Alana adjusted to motherhood very easily, and loved being a stay-at-home mom after many years as a sports massage therapist.

It was a thrill for me to be with Alana and Scott and get lots of holding time with this new baby. I was also able to be a big help to Alana as she recovered from the surgery. I made meals, cleaned up afterwards and folded a lot of laundry.

Nevan is tall like the Bristows, and very athletic. We have now started to watch some of Nevan's sports. He is involved in soccer and is also good at track and field. He is a very good student in school. He is a very polite boy and loves opportunities to be with his older cousins.

Two years after Nevan was born, Alana and Scott had another baby boy. Knowing that Alana could not deliver the baby, the doctor scheduled a Caesarean section for June 15, 2010. Once again it was seeding time on the farm, so I headed out on my own to Sexsmith, where Alana and Scott were living. For this trip, I had the phone number for the Flying J service station on the outskirts of Edmonton in my purse. I phoned to have an attendant come and fill my van with gas. Alana and Scott went to the hospital early the next morning, and I stayed with Nevan. He was a good little boy, and I managed very well with him. It wasn't long before I taught him how to get up on my lap, and I was able to change and dress him on the bed. I waited all day to hear from Scott. Finally, I got the call: they'd had another little boy, Declan. Alana was in the hospital for a couple of days. I talked to her on the phone a few times, letting her know that Nevan and I were doing fine. Once again, I was able to cuddle and hold the new baby. I was kept very busy, helping out with Nevan and making meals, cleaning up and doing laundry, while Alana recovered from her surgery. I stayed with them for about a week. Merla flew in from Calgary and drove back home with me. She was then able to spend some time with me and visit our mom at the long-term care in Outlook.

We have enjoyed Declan, our youngest grandchild. He has red hair. Many have asked where that comes from . . . it could be from my mom's side. Mom had four sisters with red hair, and Scott has some relatives with red hair. I guess it comes from both sides. We get quite a kick out of Declan's sense of humour. He has quite a personality. Grandpa loves to tease him and then blame his reaction on his red hair. He is a loving little boy. Recently, Declan stayed with us for a few days. I was trying to think of things to entertain him with at our condo. We decided to make up a bean-bag-throwing game. I made little bags that we filled with rice, as we didn't have beans. Declan made different shapes out of a big piece of cardboard that Grandpa found. He made circles, a triangle, a rectangle and a square. Each one was so many points, and he coloured them differently. We went out to the courtyard and threw our rice bags into the squares to see who got the most points. We remark often how lucky we are to have these grandchildren to add so much joy to our lives.

Our family of eight grandchildren is complete now. George and I love every opportunity to see many of their activities and have the chance to see all our grandchildren one-on-one, or all together. Alana and Scott and the boys now live in Lloydminster, only a two-and-a-half-hour drive from Saskatoon. The boys have been involved in soccer tournaments in Saskatoon, so we can continue to go to our grandchildren's sporting events.

Joseph and me making pancakes.

My granddaughter Danielle hanging off the back
of my chair. Having fun with grandkids.

My first grandkids, Donald and Susan's children,
Joseph, Danielle and Alexandra.

George and me with our second group of grandkids,
Warner, Connor and Payton.

Holding Declan with Nevan looking curious close by.

Playing ball with Declan.

All of my grandchildren.

Chapter Forty-Five

Chapter Forty-Five

Thank You for the Music

I love the Abba song that talks about being thankful for the music. The words are the way I feel. I am so thankful for music in my life. The ABBA song attests to what music means in my life. As I was growing up, music was a big part of my life, almost as big as sports. My twin sister loved music, and because Mom played the piano, music often filled our home. Gathering around the piano on Sunday evening for a singsong was a custom in our family. My younger sisters loved music too. Karen also loved to sing. We always teased Vicki about her scratchy voice, but music also filled her whole being. Musical movements and poetry recitations were some of the things that she shared in our family productions.

Merla and I were part of a junior choir in our church, and later Karen joined. Because Merla sang soprano, I was pushed into singing alto. We were often given duets to sing in Christmas programs. Merla always rose to the occasion. I usually took part when I would get serious and stop fooling around. After the junior choir, we were part of the Canadian Girls In Training choir. After moving from Preeceville, we joined the Third

Avenue United Church choir in Saskatoon. This was a big group. Merla took singing lessons in Saskatoon and was given many solos in the choir. I took a couple years of singing but didn't continue the lessons. Merla has taken lessons all of her adult life.

We all took piano lessons, and even wrote our piano exams. Mom kept us in piano for many years, and I would often beg her to let me stop, but she was determined that we would continue. I remember once, we were getting ready to do a piano exam, and we had to go to Yorkton for the test. We were to pick our time in the day when we would do our practicing at home. I always chose the morning, so that I would have the rest of the day free to play ball. My music teacher tried to convince me to give up the ball until after our piano exam, but that was impossible for me. She was afraid that I might hurt a finger and not be able to play. She knew what she was talking about, because one year I did sprain a finger just before my exam. I went for the exam anyway, with my finger taped up. We were always nervous as we waited for those piano marks to come in the mail. One particular year, Merla and her friend Gloria, who is now a gifted musician, went to the post office to see if the results were in the mail. When we got the marks, they were both in tears because they each got honours that year, but I got high-class honours. They were devastated! Merla continued her career in music, and Gloria is a very talented and successful musician. I regularly listen to Gloria on the piano at Comox United Church when she plays for their worship services. Mom always explained it by saying that the examiner must have liked a heavier touch on the keys, because I always pounded out my pieces.

After moving to Strongfield as a teacher, my music was a real asset to my teaching. I enjoyed teaching the children little songs, preparing Christmas concerts and teaching them singing games and dances. It wasn't very long before people in the United Church had me leading a junior choir. At first, I didn't think I knew much about leading a choir, but as I did it, I gained confidence and led our group for many years, giving my own children and many others the opportunity to sing and take part in operettas and musical programs. I have often said that the words of those songs would stay with them and be wonderful lessons for them all their lives, just as the words of the songs I had sung in choirs and around the piano have been with me all of mine. My children often screw up their faces when I come up with a song for some event, or out of the blue when something happens where words of a song explain the occasion. In times of joy and times of sorrow, it is a song that will lift my spirits or fill my whole being with joy.

I love the hymns that we sing each Sunday in church. It is the words and lessons from the hymns that I often take away with me as a sermon for the week. I picture myself someday running and singing praises to God at the top of my lungs with all the other saints in Heaven. I think of a song by Kurt Kaiser, "Pass It On." In the last verse, he wishes his friends could find the same happiness as he has found. He wants to climb a mountain and tell the whole world of that same happiness. The words of that verse capture the way I feel.

Chapter Forty-Six

George

"**W**here are you from? Oh, I met you when I was on SUMA board of directors," "Your son played football or hockey with my son," or, "I've seen you at the rink!" These are George's familiar questions, his way of meeting someone and striking up a conversation. George loves to meet people. He is a true extrovert and municipal politician. Even though George spent many hours alone on the tractor, he has always loved to get to know people. In a crowd, he is famous for bouncing from one group to another, getting to meet new people.

Now in our retirement, we sometimes go out for supper. George will always strike up a conversation with the young waiter or waitress by asking, "What school did you go to? Were you in sports?" Then he will tell them that his granddaughter went to that school, or his granddaughter played volleyball or basketball.

Another thing George loves is playing cards. He likes almost any card game, and he is good at them. He knows every card that has been played. When we were first married, we would play crib to see who did the dishes. I always did! We continue to play a lot of crib in the evenings. He almost always wins. Sometimes I get very frustrated, because he is also lucky.

I mentioned when I was first in the hospital that after George visited me, he visited others and always found out why they were in the hospital, where they were from and usually connected to someone they might know. He was familiar with many towns and villages in the province, and knew many of the mayors and councillors. He also got around and met the parents of the other boys who were on the teams of our sons.

When I was first in the wheelchair, George was determined that I get out and do things. He wanted me to continue to be a part of the community, and he always wanted me to accompany him to functions where other men took their wives. I joined him at almost every SUMA convention that he attended. He was a huge supporter of the things I was involved in. He would go to concerts where I led the choir, and also attended all the kids' school or Sunday school concerts. He wasn't as good at attending piano recitals, so it was me that went with Alana to music festivals and recitals. He almost always went with me when I was preaching, unless he was away, and often he sat through two services. He may have slept through one!

George was also very proud of my athletic ability, and often told people about how I ran after a fly ball in the field or hit a home run. He was a good ball player also, and we both loved the game. When we sold our house in Strongfield, Donald sold my ball glove to an antique dealer, which I was unaware of. I certainly ribbed him about selling my prize possession! One day, I was in the mall and happened to see some ball gloves in one of the sporting stores. I had to try one on. George happened to see me, and he said, "Why don't you buy it?" I said it was kind of silly for a seventy-year-old woman, in a wheelchair no less, to buy a ball glove! He encouraged me, and I bought it. I have enjoyed playing catch with Payton, Nevan and Declan. It is now one of my prize possessions.

Because I always wanted to be independent, I did whatever I could myself and very seldom asked for help, but he was always willing to help, and at the same time respected my desire to be independent. He was very proud of the things I did and supported me in every possible way. I couldn't ask for a more supportive husband, even though we often had arguments about the way I should do things, or what he thought I should or should not do! I guess we are both very stubborn and determined.

I encouraged George to go places and do things, and I was quite capable of being on my own and looking after the children. He often spent weekends away at SUMA, or at the Federation of Canadian Municipality conventions, or long days at ball tournaments. Once in a while, he'd go on a fishing trip with the guys, and once even a two-week trip to Zimbabwe with a group of four from SUMA. The province of Saskatchewan was twinned with Zimbabwe. Now, in later years, we do many things together, and as it is getting harder for me to do many things, he is always right around to help me, but rarely misses coffee row with his buddies at Market Mall.

He never complains about helping me with unpleasant things, like accidents with my bowels, things that I always did myself even if it took me a long time with a lot of effort. It is something that I hated asking him to help me with, but he never complains. He now is always willing to help. If I comment that maybe I should be in a care home or something, he scolds me and reminds me that he loves me very much, and that he said a long time ago, "for better or worse"! I have never doubted his love for me. We have a good relationship, and as we get older, the years get better. The arguments get less, and we enjoy doing things together.

Chapter Forty-Seven

Our New Home

There were a couple months during the winter that we went to Saskatoon and stayed in George's cousin's condo while she spent some time in Victoria. We enjoyed being in the city and living in a condo. George especially enjoyed the opportunity to socialize with others in the condo and play cards. He would go to hockey games and other sporting events, and I enjoyed times when we were both able to watch our grandchildren's sporting activities. It was also nice to be able to get out to the malls in the winter.

I began looking online at different condos in Saskatoon, with the idea that we might someday purchase one of our own. After Mom passed away, I saw where a condo development was to be built in the Churchill school yard after the Churchill school was torn down. This area was close to where our family lived in Saskatoon, only a few blocks away. Another thing that interested me was that it was the only condo in the area and would not be surrounded by others. It was in a residential area. I went online to see the plans of the condo. I talked to George about it, and we decided to have a look and talk to the developer, who had an office on the property before any construction had begun. We decided to put some money down, with the understanding that when construction began they would make a unit completely accessible. The same developer had built a condo in Cochrane, Alberta. We had a look at that condo and liked the plans and the idea of a courtyard that was a common area for the residents. We also liked the big open entry into the building. We kept in touch during the construction of the building to make sure there was backing in the walls for bars in the bathroom behind the toilet and the shower. We requested a roll-in shower.

George wasn't as involved as much with farming as he once was. He still owned land but didn't have as much invested in machinery. His two young cousins were making most of the decisions about the farming, and although he loved to be out on a tractor or combine, he wasn't doing as much as usual. Donald and Cameron owned land also, but they rented it out. They both had successful careers in Saskatoon.

George had also retired as mayor of the village of Strongfield in 2012, after its one-hundredth birthday, and he had served on council for over forty years. He still had a love for the village and would help out around town after he stepped down as mayor.

At the end of October in 2013, we took possession of our new condo in Saskatoon. This was the first move ever for George. He had lived in the same house he grew up in all his life. He was now ready for a new life away from Strongfield. We enjoyed that first year. We had the opportunity to watch our grandchildren in many activities: Joseph in hockey, Danni in volleyball and Alli in basketball and hockey. Warner and Connor were also getting involved in hockey and speed skating.

There were school programs that the children were involved in, Christmas concerts, band concerts and indoor track. Alana, Scott and family had moved to Lloydminster, so a trip to see their boys' activities was an easy drive. We could be back in our home and in our own beds within two and a half hours. We were kept very busy attending these events. I thought many times that I would have loved to have shown Mom our new condo. I know she would have been so pleased. In 2015, we sold our home in Strongfield, and our permanent residence became the condo in Saskatoon.

We were off to a hockey game one night when Joseph was playing in Delisle. It is nice to be in the city, and Delisle isn't very far. I couldn't remember if I had been in the rink there before, but Donald and Susan were going also, and George and Donald thought it was okay. If not, they could help me. It turned out to be just fine. I could sit behind the net and see really well next to the ice. Donald and Susan decided to stay inside the waiting room. George climbed up on the benches out near the centre line. We love to see Joseph play, as he is fun to watch. He sees the ice well and makes nice passes. He gets quite a few assists and a goal every once in a while.

I bought a fifty-fifty ticket when I got in the door. When they called the number, I checked my ticket and I was the lucky winner. They announced for the winner to collect the money up at the sound booth, but there was no way I could get up there. I waved at George, but he didn't see me. I turned around to see if Donald and Susan could see me. They were watching the game, but finally Susan saw me look around, and Donald came out. He took my ticket and got my winnings. It capped off a pretty nice evening. Joseph got a couple of assists and a goal. His team didn't win, but we enjoyed the game. It was really nice not to have to drive back to Strongfield after the game. We were soon home in our warm condo, getting out of the van in the warm underground parkade.

Warner played most of his home games at Kinsmen Arena in Saskatoon. On cold nights, I put on the heavy green jacket that I kept for hockey games. I sit in a ramped area right next to the ice. It sometimes gets cold there. Another grandma often comes and talks to me. I appreciate her friendly smile. She and her husband drive to Saskatoon from Yorkton to watch their grandson. I really appreciate not having long drives to watch our grandchildren, and I also really appreciate not having to struggle to use public washrooms. I can hurry home after the games.

When Alli was in Grade 12, she played high school basketball. We were in our condo in Saskatoon at that time. We never missed any of her games, and enjoyed watching the aggressive girls' team from St. Joseph's. They went to provincials that year and won the province. What a thrill it was for us to enjoy her final year of basketball. Our home in Saskatoon was a great place to be!

For several years, I had been taking part in the wheelchair relay for the Canadian Paraplegic Association, and I was a member of their board. I had been a member of the CPA ever since I had become a paraplegic in 1968. I always volunteered to help out where I could. I had served on the board for a few years not too long after I was awarded the honour of being Paraplegic of the Year. For many years, they held a car raffle as a fundraiser. I would volunteer two or three days to sit in one of the malls and sell tickets in Saskatoon and around the Strongfield area. The wheelchair relay became the main fundraiser after they discontinued the car raffle, and I enjoyed being involved in it. I managed to get two teams to take part for several years. Several of my friends and a couple of my grandchildren would be part of my team. We always had fun and enjoyed the event. This fed my competitive spirit, and that of some of my friends also. We did our best to win. We had a pie and coffee fundraiser in our local community, and also in Loreburn. The local people were wonderful in supporting it. Each year we raised more money. For several years we won the award for the most money raised. One year it was almost $4000. When we moved into our condo, I was still on the board, and, along with fundraisers in Strongfield and Loreburn, I canvassed for funds in the condo. People were very generous to support the Canadian Paraplegic Association, which had by then changed its name to Spinal Cord Injury Saskatchewan. Although I have retired from the board, I still support the organization.

The condo community has become our condo family in Saskatoon. We enjoy the friendships we have made, and the support from many. Soon after we moved into the condo, I met a lady who was a retired physiotherapist. We seemed to enjoy each other's company and had things in common, because of her career and my involvement with physiotherapists along with my experiences living in a wheelchair. We also shared an interest in our Christian faith and spiritual works, even though I was a member of the United Church and still involved as a licenced lay-worship leader and she was a member of the Orthodox Church. I was very interested in the spiritual things that she shared, and we enjoyed discussing different Bible passages and devotions that we had read. I even attended a conference with her at her church one time, and I found it very enlightening. There have been other friends whom we have enjoyed sharing times with in the condo. We enjoy the social times in the large common room, where we hold potluck suppers, happy hours and musical events. We have a wonderful courtyard, where we enjoy social times on nice days. We even have an exercise group that meets every weekday morning for half an hour when weather permits.

George enjoys the opportunity to go for coffee every morning with men from the condo and visit with other retirees at coffee row in Market Mall. He is always quick to volunteer to drive people to the airport or appointments if they need a ride.

In the spring of 2018, my family honoured me for my life of fifty years in the wheelchair. They invited friends and family who have shared the journey with me. We told stories of things that have happened over the years and laughed about many of the experiences.

God has showered me with the love of family and many friends, and He has led me on a journey that I may not have chosen, but it has been one of mountaintop experiences and times in the deep valleys. There are still points of deep searching in my life and many unanswered questions, but God has given me a positive attitude and the determination to be independent. I have been the best that I can be in the chair. One of my older brothers, Byron, once said, "With the cards you were dealt, you have played them well." Throughout my story, I have alluded to times that God has been present in my life. For a long time, I didn't acknowledge Him. There were times I questioned, times there were glimpses of the Spirit touching me, and then my eyes were opened to see and to begin to respond and open up to God's leading in my life. I believe that it has been God in my life leading me by the Holy Spirit. There is always more learning to do, and times that I stumble, but God has been at my side and led me all the way.

So many hymns have words that I like to share. Here's one of my favourites:

All the Way My Saviour Leads Me
By Rich Mullins

All the way my Saviour leads me
What have I to ask beside?
Can I doubt His faithful mercies?
Who through life has been my guide
Heavenly peace, divinest comfort
Ere by faith in Him to dwell
For I know whate'er fall me
Jesus doeth all things well

All of the way my Saviour leads me
Cheers each winding path I tread
Gives me strength for every trial
Feeds me with the living bread
Though my weary steps may falter
And my soul a-thirst may be
Gushing from a rock before me
Though a spirit joy I see

And all the way my Saviour leads me
Oh, the fullness of His love
Perfect rest in me is promised
In my Father's house above
When my spirit clothed immortal
Wings its flight through realms of the day
This my song through endless ages
Jesus led me all the way.

Mono ski at Whitefish.

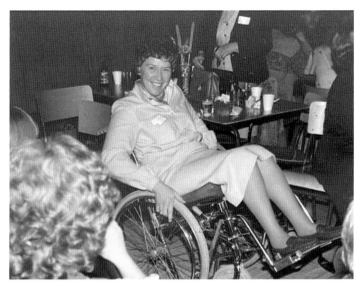

Goofing around on the chair, making others laugh.

Walking in Braces.

Driving a snowmobile—winter fun!

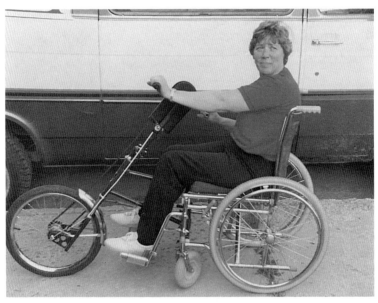

Riding my hand bicycle.

Baking with my friend Gerri for the Christmas bake sale.

George in the combine out in the field.

Carving the turkey for Christmas dinner.

Conducting the choir at church.

Receiving the Queen's Jubilee Medal.

George and me outside our home in Strongfield.

My siblings, Karen, Vicki, Kent and Merla.

George and me.

Our kids and their spouses.

Donald and Susan.

Cameron and Devre.

Alana and Scott.

Our big, happy family.

About the Author

Mavis Bristow is a daughter, sister, wife, educator, mother, and grandma. She has been devoted to a life of faith and happily shares how it impacted her journey within this book. Mavis studied Education at the Teachers College and University of Saskatchewan, then went on to earn her Certificate in Theology. Her studies and life experiences are what led her to writing All The Way. She and her husband, George, live in Saskatoon, Saskatchewan, surrounded by family and friends.

Mavis

Testimonials

"Mavis is one of my hero's. Her humility, warmth, and genuine personality are only exceeded by her resiliency and determination. Despite facing the personal and societal challenges of being a paraplegic in a less than accessible world for much of her more than 50 years in a wheelchair, Mavis has been a true leader and force for change, making the world a better (and more accessible) place. On top of that, she makes great cookies."

Mitch Dahl BScPT, Sport PT

"I met Mavis in spring of 2006 and that meeting changed my life. I had returned from the International Seating Symposium and had a new product, the Ride Designs Custom Cushion, of which I knew next to nothing. Mavis, being a woman of many firsts, had already researched this cushion and was very interested in it. From that meeting began a lifelong friendship, both professional and personal, that I cherish to this day. It changed the trajectory of my professional career, resulting in this cushion being put on our government program and changing the lives of hundreds of people. If Mavis hadn't believed in this cushion, and in me, I truly believe that many of my clients would not be alive today. And for that I am eternally grateful to her".

Pat Molloy
Rehab Equipment Specialist
Ride Designs Custom Seating Provider (Cert.2006, 2015)

As owners of a local Funeral Home, we have had the privilege of knowing Mavis for over 30 years. We have always been encouraged by her willingness to serve others. Families trust her to come alongside them in their times of grief. Her wheelchair does not keep her from ministering, be it speaking or counselling those who request her care. We will always be amazed at her ability to face and meet the challenges that have been placed in her way and to do so with a quiet spirit and a willing heart. Mavis has been a blessing in our lives.

Floyd & Marjorie Childerhose
Outlook Funeral Chapel

Mavis is someone I look up to as I was paralyzed myself in my early 20s and I know Mavis through my grandparents that were from Loreburn before they both passed away. When I was first injured I asked Mavis for advice and I appreciated her insights. It was reassuring to me knowing that I could have a family some day and have a good life knowing that Mavis was able to have a family and live a good life when accessibility wasn't as important in society as it is now. I can only imagine the hardships she faced when she was first injured and I respect her good attitude which is key in life.

Ryan Orton

My Granddaughter, Danielle

‑‑‑‑‑‑‑‑‑∞∞∞‑‑‑‑‑‑‑‑‑

Hello readers. For those of you who made it here, let me introduce myself. My name is Danielle and I am the eldest granddaughter of my grandma and grandpa's bunch. I share a large passion for writing and storytelling with my grandma, so when she asked me to help her with her book publishing process I was greatly honoured. My Grandma and I had a lot of fun reminiscing on old times and I enjoyed getting to discuss all of the events that she discusses in her book. It felt like VIP access to an authors book reading. As you now know after reading this book, my grandma is an incredible women and she is one of my biggest inspirations.

My grandma asked that I include a little bit about myself to introduce readers to the sous-chef of the her book publishing journey. So here we go. Although pictured earlier on in the book as a young nugget hanging from the back of her wheelchair, I am now in my mid-twenties trying to get creative with my own navigation of the world. After graduating from my Communications, Culture and Journalism studies program I started a media and brand development company that allowed me to blend my love of people, communications and design. I now own an independent business based out of Saskatoon called **Radiate.** I build creative products, invest in new ideas, and help companies grow their brand. I work with companies on logo design, brand strategy & identity, digital web design, social media consulting, content creation and communications. My focus is a blend of client needs and innovative design that goes together to deliver seamless, personalized and enjoyable service sure to exceed all expectations. I really love what I do.

The last thing I will share is the inspiration behind the front cover of this book. I have always loved to draw and paint. I think this may have stemmed from my childhood, as my grandma was always making crafts and puppets and games for us to play. At the beginning of the publishing process, my grandma asked that I would be the one to design the front cover and gave me complete artistic freedom. Again, I felt so lucky to be chosen. I wanted the front cover to be inspired by softball. My grandma has always loved the game and when she plays catch with you, you can see the passion in her eyes and the enjoyment in her smile. Behind the book title you can see an old scoreboard, and my grandma is facing that direction reminiscing about the field she used to play on. This moment is meant to symbolize her story writing process and the way this book reflects on all the stories that have taken place throughout her life.

That's it from me. I hope you are filled to the brim with inspiration from my grandma's book and that you walk away with a new perspective. She is a wonderful person and I feel endlessly grateful that I have had her as a strong role model to look up to throughout my life. Grandma, I love you and I am so thankful for all that you have taught me.

Danielle, owner of Radiate.

For more information about Radiate,
visit www.raddesignhouse.com